POETIC TRUTH

Poetry
Patmos and Other Poems (1955)
Third Day Lucky (1958)
Two Ballads of the Muse (1960)
Begging the Dialect (1960)
The Dark Window (1962)
An Irish Gathering (1964)
A Ballad of Billy Barker (1965)
Inscriptions (1967)
Because of This (1968)
Selected Poems 1947–1967 (1968)
An Irish Album (1969)
Georges Zuk : Selected Verse (1969)
Answers (1969)
The Hunting Dark (1971)
Two Hundred Poems from the Greek Anthology (1971)
A Different Mountain (1972)
A Private Speech (1972)
Musebook (1972)
Three for Herself (1972)
Country Songs (1973)
Timelight (1974)
Georges Zuk: The Underwear of the Unicorn (1975)
Callsigns (1976)
Because of Love (1977)
Three Poems (1977)

Books About Poetry
The Poetic Pattern (1956)
The Practice of Poetry (1971)
The Poet's Calling (1975)

Editions of Poetry
J. M. Synge : Collected Poems (1962)
Selected Poems of Byron (1965)
David Gascoyne : Collected Poems (1965)
David Gascoyne : Collected Verse Translations (with Alan Clodd) (1970)

Anthologies
Viewpoint : An Anthology of Poetry (1962)
Six Irish Poets (1962)
Poetry of the Thirties (1964)
Five Poets of the Pacific Northwest (1964)
Poetry of the Forties (1968)
The Cavalier Poets (1970)

POETIC TRUTH

by

Robin Skelton

HEINEMANN
LONDON

BARNES & NOBLE
NEW YORK

THE BOOK SOCIETY OF CANADA
AGINCOURT

Heinemann Educational Books Ltd

LONDON EDINBURGH MELBOURNE AUCKLAND TORONTO
HONG KONG SINGAPORE KUALA LUMPUR IBADAN NAIROBI
JOHANNESBURG LUSAKA NEW DELHI KINGSTON

U.K. edition
ISBN 0 435 18821 6 (cased)
ISBN 0 435 18822 4 (paper)

U.S. edition
ISBN 0-06-496253-9 (cloth)
ISBN 0-06-496252-0 (paper)

Canadian edition
ISBN 1-7725-5278-9

Published in Great Britain by
Heinemann Educational Books Ltd
48 Charles Street, London W1X 8AH
Published in the U.S.A. 1978 by
Harper & Row Publishers, Inc.
Barnes & Noble Import Division
Set by Eta Services (Typesetters) Ltd, Beccles, Suffolk
Printed by William Clowes & Sons, Limited
London, Colchester and Beccles

Contents

Acknowledgements

The author and publishers wish to thank the following for permission to reproduce copyright material:

Alfred A. Knopf Inc. for Section XII from 'An Ordinary Evening in New Haven' (c) 1950 by Wallace Stevens and 'Thirteen Ways of Looking at a Blackbird' (c) 1923 and renewed 1951 by Wallace Stevens, from *The Collected Poems of Wallace Stevens*; Oxford University Press Inc. for 'The Combat', 'Too Much' and the extract from 'Variations on a Time Theme' from *Collected Poems* by Edwin Muir (c) by Willa Muir; Deborah Rogers Ltd and The Hogarth Press Ltd for 'Waiting for the Barbarians' from *The Poems of C. P. Cavafy*, translated by John Mavrogordato; Jonathan Cape Ltd and the Estate of Robert Frost for 'The Road Not Taken' and 'Design' from *The Poetry of Robert Frost*, edited by Edward Connery Lathem; Farrar, Straus & Giroux Inc. for 'The Republic' from *History* by Robert Lowell (c) 1973 by Robert Lowell, and for 'Dream Song 112' from *The Dream Songs* by John Berryman (c) 1959, 1962, 1963, 1964, 1965, 1966, 1967, 1968, 1969 by John Berryman; Faber & Faber Ltd for the extracts from *Deviation into Sense* by O. S. Wauchope, for the extract from *The Waste Land* and the extract from 'Tradition and the Individual Talent' from *Selected Essays* by T. S. Eliot, for 'Thirteen Ways of Looking at a Blackbird' from *The Collected Poems of Wallace Stevens*, for 'The Combat', 'Too Much' and the extract from 'Variations on a Time Theme' from *Collected Poems* by Edwin Muir, for 'The Republic' from *History* by Robert Lowell, for 'Summer Song II' from *Collected Poems* by George Barker, for 'Loss' from *The Father Found* by Charles Madge, and for 'Dream Song 112' from *His Toy, His Dream, His Rest* by John Berryman; Harcourt Brace Jovanovich Inc. for the extract from *The Waste Land* and for the extract from 'Tradition and the Individual Talent' from *Selected Essays* by T. S. Eliot, (c) 1932, 1936, 1950 by Harcourt Brace Jovanovich Inc., (c) 1960, 1964 by T. S. Eliot, for 'anyone lived in a pretty how town' from *Complete Poems 1913–1962* by e.e. cummings, (c) 1940 by e.e. cummings, (c) 1968 by Marion Morehouse Cummings, and for the extract from *Saving the Appearances* by Owen Barfield; Routledge & Kegan Paul Ltd for the extracts from *Principles of Literary Criticism* by I. A. Richards, for the extracts from *Articulate Energy* by Donald Davie, and for the extracts from *Feeling and Form* by Susanne Langer, for the extracts from *Speculations* by T. E. Hulme; Houghton Mifflin Company for 'Ars Poetica' from *Collected Poems 1917–1952* by Archibald MacLeish (c) 1952 by Archibald MacLeish; The Trustees of the Hardy Estate, Macmillan London and Basingstoke and The Macmillan Company of Canada for 'On the Way' from *The New Wessex Edition of The Complete Poems of Thomas Hardy*; Michael Butler Yeats, Miss Anne Yeats, Macmillan London and Basingstoke and Macmillan Publishing Co. Inc. for the extract from 'The Apparitions' (c) 1940 by Georgie Yeats, 1968 by Bertha Georgie Yeats, Michael Butler Yeats and Anne Yeats, for the extract from 'Sailing to Byzantium' (c) 1928 by Macmillan Publishing Co. Inc. renewed 1956 by Georgie Yeats, for the extract from 'The Second Coming' (c) 1924 by Macmillan Publishing Co. Inc. renewed 1952 by Bertha Georgie Yeats, all poems from *Collected Poems* by William Butler Yeats; Dame Edith Sitwell, Macmillan London and Basingstoke and Vanguard Press Inc. for the extract from 'The Song of the Cold' from *Collected Poems* by Edith Sitwell; MacGibbon & Kee Ltd/Granada Publishing Ltd for 'anyone lived in a pretty how town' from *Complete Poems 1913–1962* by e.e. cummings; Stephen H. Fritchman for 'Hasbrouck and the Rose' from *The Five Seasons* by Phelps Putnam; Charles Scribner's Sons for extracts from *Feeling and Form* by Susanne Langer; Robert Graves for 'The Persian Version' from *The Collected Poems of Robert Graves*; Doubleday & Company for the extract from 'Linguistics and Poetics' by Roman Jacobson in *The Structuralists from Marx to Lévi-Strauss* by Richard T. and Fernande De George (c) 1972 by Richard T. and Fernande De George; Oxford University Press for the extracts from *The Nature of Experience* by Sir Russell Brain (c) 1959 Oxford University Press, for Section XII from 'For a Lost Girl' from *With Love Somehow* by Tony Connor (c) 1962 Oxford University Press; Hodder & Stoughton for the extract from *Teach Yourself Poetry* by Robin Skelton; Victor Gollancz Ltd for the extract from 'Notes for a Commentary on Milton' by Northrop Frye, and the extract from 'The Little Girl Lost and Found and The Lapsed Soul' by Kathleen Raine, both from *In the Divine Vision, Studies in the Poetry and Art of William Blake*, edited by Vivian de Sola Pinto; The Modern Language Association of America for the extract from *The Historical Criticism of Milton* by A. S. P. Woodhouse (PMLA 1951); Mr Owen Barfield for the extract from *Saving the Appearances*; Mr Alastair Reid for his poem 'A Game of Glass' from *Oddments, Etchings, Moments*; The Keio University, Institute of Cultural and Linguistic Studies, Tokyo for the extracts from *Language and Magic* by Toshihiko Izutsu; Garnstone Press Ltd/Geoffrey Bles Ltd for the extracts from *The Destiny of Man* translated by Natalie Duddington and from *Truth and Revelation* translated by R. M. French, both by Nicolas Berdyaev.

Preface

This is the third in a series of three books about the nature of poetry and the poetic experience which I began working on over ten years ago. In the first of my trilogy I was concerned with the art and craft of poetry, and attempted to show how it is made and to do so, as far as possible, in a fashion that might make the book of use to would-be writers of poetry. This book, *The Practice of Poetry* (1971), I followed with a second book in which I attempted to describe the poet's way of life, the nature of his (or her) vocation, and the kind of disciplines and difficulties endemic to the profession. *The Poet's Calling* (1975) avoided theory as resolutely as did *The Practice of Poetry*. I was concerned in both of these books to present facts rather than arguments, and bring forward as many witnesses as possible, without deducing any conclusions from their statements. Finally, in this book, I have attempted to present the *Poetic Truth* as I see it. This is therefore a book of speculations and conclusions, and while it does not require the reader to have glanced at the two other books which preceded it, it does, I hope, suggest answers to problems posed or implied by those books and in no way contradicts the evidence they present. It is, like its predecessors, a personal book. By this I mean that I have not attempted to gather all the various poetic theories about the nature of poetry together and set them at each other's throats. I have chosen rather to ignore theories which I find unsatisfactory than to set them up as Aunt Sallies in order to knock them down, and I have made use of quotations from the work of other writers only when it seems to me that they have something to say which is essential to the development of my own argument. The list of my omissions is horrendous. I have not quoted Longinus or Coleridge. I have kept clear of Burke and Wimsatt. I have evaded Cassirer, and spared only an oblique glance for Herbert Read. Eccentrically, I have chosen to claim assistance from such other rarely adduced writers (at least in this context) as Berdyaev and Pierre Emmanuel, and have supported my argument by despicably selective quotations from John Dewey, Susanne Langer and I. A. Richards. I have skated happily, if sometimes clumsily, upon thin ice in crossing such dangerously deep waters as those labelled 'history of language' and 'origins of speech'. I have sped past Bergson and have skirted both existentialism and neoplatonism. If I were capable of blushing, I would blush.

Nevertheless, it has seemed to me that this rather cavalier approach was necessary if I was not to present a book of such appalling weight and complexity as to daunt the reader and alarm the publisher, and if I was not to fall into the academic elephant trap which is laid across the path of every seeker after truth, and which causes weighty arguments to crash to sudden destruction when they are but a little way on the road to discovery. I would rather present an inadequately ponderable argument that arrived at a conclusion than a ponderous one which arrived nowhere.

There will be—there must, and there should be—doubts as to whether I have reached any satisfactory goal in my journey. I confess to having one or two doubts myself, for there are of necessity many questions left unanswered and any competent writer could write a full-length book about any one of them. I am tempted by one or two of them myself. On the other hand, I find myself recalling just how often in the history of ideas it has been the initial sketch, the preliminary 'paper', that has, for all its obvious and confessed inadequacies, stimulated new theories and discoveries to a greater extent than the ensuing, and usually long-delayed, full-length study, and comfort myself with the hope that while *Poetic Truth* may not convince as gospel, it might serve as goad.

The University of Victoria,   R.S.
British Columbia.

ONE Words in Space

It is necessary, first of all, to establish certain facts concerning the 'Poetic Process', taking this phrase as referring equally to the experience of the poet while writing and the experience of the reader when most fully apprehending any given poem. Let us deal with the poet's view first. It has often been pointed out that the poet, in the act of writing, is almost never using only his conscious intelligence. It appears to him that his conscious ratiocinative mind is augmented by promptings from the depths of his unconscious, and that all his faculties of perception—instinctual, emotional, cerebral, and sensual—are operating as a unity. He experiences a sense of freedom and power which never comes to him at non-creative moments. The war between the imagined and the real has ended. All mental events have equal validity, though not, of course, equal importance. His sense of time is affected. He not only feels at moments of extreme creative vitality as if he has escaped from time into a condition of being which, in its concentrated total awareness of all phenomena as vital and personally enriching (though the sense of possessing a distinct and separate individuality is often noticeably absent) reveals man at his highest potentiality, but is also able to perceive in a *spatial* fashion. That is to say that, whereas normally a word appears to have a distinct single meaning and a series of possible variations and associations, and must be used in such a way that only one or two of these possibilities are evoked, now the word seems to operate as a unity of all its powers. It is supposed that normally one must perceive in terms of language by constantly selecting one focal meaning or significance for each word and using it with precision: now the word is a 'portmanteau'; it contains many personal, historical, and imaginative associations. The word 'stone' for instance is itself a whole collection of stones, a whole library of anthropological references, and a whole volume of literary references, and yet operates as a unity. It is immensely manipulatable, and it is its kinetic as much as its pleromatic quality which excites the mind. The reason for referring to this perception of the word as spatial may need explanation. Since we are discussing not achieved poetry, but the state of mind which makes poetry possible, an elementary example may be sufficient. Let us suppose that in this heightened condition of awareness the poet finds the following sentence come into his head: 'The red ball fell from the child's torn hand.' It is obvious that all the words in this sentence with the exception of the definite article and the word 'from' have associative possibilities. One might list them as follows:

(The)	red	blood (thus sacrifice, wound and life)	} sunset, bloody world
	ball	mandala, world sun, spinning	
	fell	failure, the Fall of Man, descent (as avatar)	} the world created or discarded
(from the)	child's	innocence, ignorance, weakness, simplicity, Christ, Out of the mouths of babes, birth	} by Christ, or by innocence, or by the state of childhood
	torn	wounded (by malice or accident), Christ's hands, the wounded hero	
	hand	the making part of the body, the potter's hand	

To read this statement in this fashion is to read 'spatially'. The sentence has several meanings, but these are not differentiated. The statement exists as a statement in the same way that a picture exists as a total visual impression. The eye accepts the picture as one thing. It may contain many different shapes and colours, but the impact is of the total unity. The unity is however made up of shapes and colours which direct the eye to move in many directions, and which may, for many reasons, have associative powers, either simply visual or more cerebral, which 'lie behind' the total effect. In the same way as a picture is a unity composed of many shapes and colours disposed in space, so is the word to the poet at the moment of writing. And analysis of the word's composition comes after the word has been written, and not before.

If we are to call this perception a 'spatial' one, we may perhaps contrast it with a more usual notion of language by using the word 'linear'. Language that moves, not in depth and by means of units of immense pleromatic and kinetic power, but by means of precise denotation exclusive of all but accidental ambiguity, is related to 'spatial' language in the same way that a straight line is related to an area. A straight line is the shortest distance between two points, and has direction but not magnitude. An area is possessed of magnitude. It is the difference between the notion of a road as a means of transport from one place to another, and a road as a means of enabling one to exist at the centre of a landscape, perceived as complex and interesting, and which alters continually as one moves.

In picking the sentence, 'The red ball fell from the child's torn hand' I have, of course, chosen an extreme and perhaps ludicrous example of the poet's 'spatial' experience of language. It is clear that in the writing of most poems the poet will perceive some words in a more spatial fashion than others, and it is also clear that not all poems, or even all parts of any one poem, will be written (or read) with the same awareness of spatial elements. Take, for example, Alastair Reid's poem, *A Game of Glass*.[1]

> I do not believe this room
> with its cat and its chandelier,
> its chessboard-tiled floor,
> and its shutters that open out
> on an angel playing a fountain,
> and the striped light slivering in
> to a room that looks the same
> in the mirror over my shoulder,
> with a second glass-eyed cat.
>
> My book does not look real.
> The room and the mirror seem
> to be playing a waiting game.
> The cat has made its move,
> the fountain has one to play,
> and the thousand eyes of the angel
> in the chandelier above
> gleam beadily, and say
> the next move is up to me.

[1] In Paul Engle and Joseph Langland (eds.), *Poets' Choice*, The Dial Press, 1962, pp. 242–3.

How can I trust my luck ?
Whatever way I look,
I cannot tell which is the door,
and I do not know who is who—
the thin man in the mirror,
or the watery one in the fountain.
The cat is eyeing my book.
What am I meant to do ?
Which side is the mirror on ?

While the title suggests complexity and multiple meaning, the opening lines, even though affected by the first line's expression of doubt, are factual enough for us to read them in a linear manner. When, however, we reach the angel playing the fountain we are forced to think and feel spatially, to recognize that there are powerful associations here and that they form an essential part of the poem. By the time we reach the end of the poem we are in a world where the linear procedures of factual truth and logic no longer apply.

Alastair Reid has described the writing of this poem, and while his description does not involve an examination of the change from linear to spatial use of language it does vividly present the way in which a linear approach to phenomena was overcome by a spatial one.[1]

'A Game of Glass' is the one poem of mine which *occurred* to me, as an actual happening—the only thing I had to do was to catch it and hold it in words as clearly as possible.

I was sitting in my workroom in Spain, one morning very early, writing. The room was exactly as reconstituted in the poem—a large mirror on the wall behind me, shutters in front of me opening to the fountained garden, a huge chandelier, a black and white tiled floor, and my writing table in the middle. All at once, I looked up, and caught the eyes of the cat gazing at me intently—and I felt, for an endless moment, a realisation of utter mystery, in which I existed in no familar sense, but was simply one element in a vast, inexplicable game, which the cat understood more completely than I. There was something of Through the Looking Glass about it ; the feeling was awesome. The coinciding reflections, the chessboard, the un-recognition, all sustained the moment ; the poem followed almost at once. I cannot be sure that my profound astonishment is properly contained in it ; but I do know that whenever I happen to read it over, I re-enter the moment most vividly, as more than a memory.

Except in the manner of its happening, the poem is not out of key with the rest of my work, since to explore the amazement of finding myself alive has

[1] ibid., p. 243.

been my preoccupation. But this poem reassures me ; through it, I can feel beyond words to the happening itself, and realise always that the mystery *does* exist, prior to them.

The 'mystery' to which Reid refers is, obviously, that of the nature of man and of his place in the universe. It is also the mystery of man's occasional, and often startling, perception of something beyond or within the ordinary surroundings and happenings of common experience. It is the mystery of that movement from linear to spatial perception which astonishes us when we read:

> To be or not to be. That is the question:
> Whether 'tis nobler in the mind to suffer
> *The slings and arrows of outrageous fortune*

It is the mystery to which Thomas Sharp referred when he wrote in his poem, *Roots*:[1]

> I've known days when a passing sight
> Was window to the infinite

It is also the mystery which both Edward Carpenter and Mark Rutherford encountered in terms of trees. Their accounts express extremely well the way in which one's vision can quite suddenly take on new and strange dimensions, the one object becoming almost a universe in itself.[2]

Has any one of us ever *seen* a Tree ? I certainly do not think that I have—except most superficially. That very penetrating observer and naturalist, Henry D. Thoreau, tells us he would often make an appointment to visit a certain tree, miles away—but what or whom he saw when he got there, he does not say. Walt Whitman, also a keen observer . . . mentions that, in a dream trance he actually once saw his 'favourite trees step out and promenade up, down and around, *very curiously*'. Once the present writer seemed to have a partial vision of a tree. It was a beech, standing somewhat isolated, and still leafless in quite early Spring. Suddenly I was aware of its skyward-reaching arms and up-turned finger-tips, as if some vivid life (or electricity) was streaming through them far into the spaces of heaven, and of its roots plunged in the earth and drawing the same energies from below. The day was quite still and there was no movement in the branches, but in that moment the tree was no longer a separate or separable organism, but a vast being ramifying far into space, sharing and uniting the life of Earth and Sky, and full of most amazing activity. . . .

EDWARD CARPENTER

[1] In Walter de la Mare, *Behold, This Dreamer*, Faber and Faber, 1939, p. 533.
[2] ibid., pp. 529–30.

One morning when I was in the wood something happened which was nothing less than a transformation of myself and the world, although I 'believed' nothing new. I was looking at a great, spreading, bursting oak. The first tinge from the greenish-yellow buds was just visible. It seemed to be no longer a tree away from me and apart from me. The enclosing barriers of consciousness were removed and the text came into my mind, 'Thou in me and I in Thee.' The distinction of self and not-self was an illusion. I could feel the rising sap; in me also sprang the fountain of life up-rushing from its roots, and the joy of its outbreak at the extremity of each twig right up to the summit was my own: that which kept me apart was nothing. . . .

MARK RUTHERFORD

While we are here presented with two experiences that some might call mystical we must not forget that we are presented with them in *language*. The words provide us with the experience, though Carpenter and Rutherford, as they were not writing poems when they had their visions, experienced their altered sense of the nature of the tree by non-verbal means. It is, however, clear that the word 'tree' itself is one that lends itself easily to spatial perception, for (as Carpenter's account suggests) the image of the tree has many associations, and a large number of these are with religious and historical matters that themselves reverberate with multiple possibilities of meaning. One thinks, immediately, of the tree upon which Christ hung, of the tree of the Hesperides, of the sacred trees and groves of many people in many lands.

Some words, obviously, have more potential spatial 'range' than others. There is a considerable difference between the potential spatial reach of a word like 'blood' and a word like 'saucepan'. The poet as he writes is aware of the different intensities of words. There is a widening and narrowing of associative possibilities. Sometimes a word stands out sharp, clear, and particular, having no background, no 'surround', at all. The object, and only the object, is in focus. On the other hand, sometimes, while the object is clearly in focus, the territory of which it is the centre is also clearly seen. And, again, it is possible for the object to be blurred, imprecise, out of focus, while the country in which it is situated is clear and important. This alteration in 'focality' gives the poem that sense of altering dimensions without which it could not correspond to the nature of human perception, for our progress through life is attended always by these movements of expansion and contraction, these alterations of scale and intensity. If we are to discuss these variations with any accuracy, however, we must label the three main kinds of focality. Let us call the image which is clear and definite, and which clearly suggests a

whole territory of qualities, images, and ideas, a case of 'total focality'.
The image which is clear in itself, but which has no background of
important associations, we may refer to as having a 'short focus', and
that which is blurred, while having an important surround or aura we
may think of having a 'long focus'. Consequently 'holy' we might find
to be 'long focus', 'kettle' to be 'short focus', and 'blood' to have 'total
focality'.

This series of distinctions is useless as an implement outside particular
poems, of course. Words are indications and not definitions, and their
meanings and their focality are controlled by their positioning in a
linguistic whole. In one context a word which we would ordinarily regard
as 'short focus' may turn out to have total focality. The word phrase
'coat upon a coat-hanger', for example, would seem to be very short
focus indeed and also a linear kind of language but W. B. Yeats gave it
total focus in his poem, *The Apparitions*.[1]

Because there is safety in derision
I talked about an apparition,
I took no trouble to convince,
Or seem plausible to a man of sense,
Distrustful of that popular eye
Whether it be bold or sly.
Fifteen apparitions have I seen;
The worst a coat upon a coat-hanger.

I have found nothing half so good
As my long-planned half solitude,
Where I can sit up half the night
With some friend that has the wit
Not to allow his looks to tell
When I am unintelligible.
Fifteen apparitions have I seen;
The worst a coat upon a coat-hanger.

When a man grows old his joy
Grows more deep day after day,
His empty heart is full at length,
But he has need of all that strength
Because of the increasing Night
That opens her mystery and fright.
Fifteen apparitions have I seen;
The worst a coat upon a coat-hanger.

[1] W. B. Yeats, *Collected Poems*, Macmillan, 1950, pp. 386–7.

Yeats achieves this total focality for the coat on the coat-hanger by juxtaposing that image with more intense and abstract statements so that, because of its positioning in the poem, the one short focus phrase takes unto itself all the associations provided by the other words in the poem, all of which are long focus, abstractions and blurred in outline— what I have called elsewhere diffuse images.

Another instance of the way in which the poem can use altering focality, and proceed from a linear to a spatial statement is Robert Frost's *The Road Not Taken*.[1]

> Two roads diverged in a yellow wood,
> And sorry I could not travel both
> And be one traveller, long I stood
> And looked down one as far as I could
> To where it bent in the undergrowth;
>
> Then took the other, as just as fair,
> And having perhaps the better claim,
> Because it was grassy and wanted wear;
> Though as for that the passing there
> Had worn them really about the same,
>
> And both that morning equally lay
> In leaves no step had trodden black.
> Oh, I kept the first for another day!
> Yet knowing how way leads on to way,
> I doubted if I should ever come back.
>
> I shall be telling this with a sigh
> Somewhere ages and ages hence:
> Two roads diverged in a wood, and I—
> I took the one less travelled by,
> And that has made all the difference.

The first two verses appear entirely linear. The images are short focus and several of them are somewhat diffuse, being rather generalized and imprecise, like 'undergrowth', 'yellow wood', 'grassy', 'traveller'. The third verse, by its contemplative tone, suggests that perhaps there is more significance in the experience than meets the eye. The fourth verse, by suddenly introducing the perspective of time with the line 'Somewhere ages and ages hence', alters the whole poem. Because up to this point the

---

[1] *Complete Poems of Robert Frost*, Jonathan Cape, 1951, p. 129.

language has been sturdily and yet unemphatically factual we accept the phrase 'ages and ages' as meaning exactly what it says, as being a reference to a length of time well beyond the normal life span. As a consequence, and paradoxically, we now read the image of the road as metaphor or parable because we have been forced to accept the earlier part of the poem as fact, and to believe in the linear nature of the statements. At the end we find ourselves re-experiencing the whole of the poem in terms at least of allegory, but (because there are no precise intellectual equivalents provided for each of the images) most probably as parable, as a story with many associations and meanings.

Frost's method in *The Road Not Taken* is extremely subtle; Yeats' in *The Apparitions* is much more crude. Both poets have, however, utilized the difference between linear and spatial perception, and both have made use of the notion of focality, Yeats by means of a simple and dramatic contrast, Frost by means of a sudden presentation of one long focus line at a strategic point in a poem which till that moment had appeared to be short focus.

It is not easy to be precise about the degrees of focality, for much depends upon the sensibility of the individual reader. It is, however, possible to see that shifting focality is characteristic of poetry and that in what we recognize as poetry or poetic writing the shifting focalities invariably include words of such long focus that the piece of writing has to be regarded as operating in a spatial and not a linear fashion.

It could, indeed, be argued that the difference between non-poetic verse and poetic verse can be perceived in terms of the work's spatial qualities. For example, I would maintain that the following is merely verse:[1]

> Proud Preston, poor people,
> Eight bells in a cracked steeple

whereas this similar couplet is poetry:[2]

> River of Dart, O river of Dart,
> Every year thou claimest a heart

I chose these two examples to make the further point that verse may sometimes be more satisfying than poetry. The spatial element in the second poem arrives only out of the employment of the reverberant

---

[1] In Geoffrey Grigson (ed.), *The Faber Book of Popular Verse*, Faber and Faber, 1971, p. 129.
[2] ibid., p. 172.

word 'heart' and the luckily equally suggestive name of the river. The first couplet is trenchant without being spatial, at least for this particular reader.

Once we have recognized the 'portmanteau' or spatial nature of many words in poetry, and once we have proposed that one of the differences between poetry and non-poetry can be defined in terms of degrees of focality, we must decide whether or not this use of language bears any resemblance to the ordinary man's attitude towards words. It is obvious that ordinary conversation depends to a considerable extent upon the recognition of ambiguities and multiple implications, but this could simply mean that conversation often aspires to the condition of poetry, and leave us still with the conviction that the 'poetic' method is a special case. We usually regard words as being stable, and consider any evidence of instability as being an intrusion of some anarchic spirit into the language system; this spirit is devoted to the cracking of jokes, the contriving of puns, the confusing of arguments, the intensifying of misunderstandings, and, of course, the writing of 'poetry'. There is something to be said for this attitude, in that the employment of portmanteau and focality techniques, to a greater extent than that accepted by habitual vernacular usage, does lead to language departing from that system of precise denotations so usefully created by the lexicographer. The error in the argument, however, lies in the supposition that a system coherent within itself and dependent upon precise delimitations is, because more useful as a working implement than a less coherent and precise system, also more true to the facts. This error leads to the general acceptance of a dogma in preference to a revelation, a definition in preference to an indication, a moral code in preference to a religious faith. We must, however, remember that every dictionary definition, and moral code, is made by man in order to reduce the true complexity of the situation to manipulatable proportions, and that the very existence of dictionaries, codes, and definitions implies a degree of selection and, therefore, distortion. Moreover, the 'working system' is often known to be a gross approximation, even while it is, for utilitarian purposes, accepted as accurate. The nature of time is, of course, a case in point. The scientist is aware that clock-time is not true to the nature of the time-space continuum, but he continues to regulate his day by his watch, rather than by the discoveries of Einstein.

Once these ideas have been stated, we can perhaps examine the situation without supposing that anything which does not fit with an accepted system is necessarily an aberration, as it is quite possible that the system itself is a departure from the facts. Let us therefore look again at this question of stability. Heinz Werner has indicated the difference between semantically stable and semantically unstable words. He wrote,[1]

> A semantically stable word is clearly identifiable in varying contexts due to four characteristics: (a) specificity of expression: the range of acceptable substitutes (synonymity) for the word is small; (b) semantic constancy: variability of content (homonymity) is small; (c) definiteness of meaning: word boundary is sharp, that is, the 'fringe of associations' that diffusely accompanies the semantic core of the word is small; (d) articulateness of meaning: the word as a meaningful unit is relatively self-contained with respect to the context in which it stands. Conversely then, instability of word meaning is definable in terms of a lack of those characteristics: a word is the less stable in its meaning, and therefore, the more susceptible to change (a) the less specific the content expressed by it, (b) the more numerous the shades of its meaning, (c) the more diffuse and wider its associative fringe, and (d) the more it is fused with or embedded in the context within which it stands.

Consequently, according to Professor Werner, the more 'portmanteau' quality a word possesses, and the 'longer' or more nearly 'total' its focus, the more it is liable to suffer semantic change.

We are not, however, concerned with semantic change as such, though it might be as well to comment here that almost all words alter the nature of their associative surround as time proceeds. The exceptions are those words coined entirely for purposes of definition, words such as 'chromosome', or 'chloride'. Even these words, once they have become part of the general vocabulary and have been used figuratively or associated with important events, can develop powerful associations however. One has only to consider how the emotional implications of the words 'hydrogen' and 'cog' have increased over a short period; once a hydrogen bomb was made, and once a man had described himself as 'only a cog in the machine', a change in connotation had occurred. It is, however, true that 'semantically most stable words are those of highly developed scientific terminologies. . . .' Apart from these, there are very few words indeed which are as stable as the general reader tends to believe, and even fewer which lack any observable associative surround.

[1] Heinz Werner, 'Change of Meaning: A Study of Semantic Processes Through the Experimental Method', *Journal of General Psychology*, 1954, 50, 181–208, p. 182.

We can, therefore, agree that when a poem uses a word in such a way that it is plurivalent in meaning, it is not running counter to the nature of language, but making obvious one of its most basic characteristics. Nevertheless, it is a far cry from a word with a small associative surround to a 'portmanteau' word. Here we may well feel that poetic language is running to extremes of eccentricity. Werner develops this point for us.[1]

> For the highly literate person who knows his grammar, a word is a lexical unit, a building block, as it were, for the construction of a sentence; it is an element, sufficiently circumscribed in meaning to be placed, with similar elements, into an ordered pile, called a dictionary. However, at less advanced, more concrete planes of speech the word does not possess that lexical, elemental character because of two reasons: (a) It possesses, to a greater or lesser degree, a 'holophrastic' meaning, i.e., a meaning which can be conveyed explicitly only by a whole phrase or even a series of phrases. Extreme forms of holophrastic speech can be well observed in early language, holophrastic words that stand for broad, affective and perceptual associations abound also in the speech of primitive man; they are apparent in the talk of low-educated people within our own own culture; furthermore, holophrasis is a characteristic feature of slang, as well as of emotional language even of highly literate people; and finally, holophrastic expressions are conspicuous in certain abnormal conditions such as dreams, schizophrenia, hysteria, etc. (b) The word, on a less differentiated speech level, does not possess the relative independence from the larger speech units in which it is used. Its content is profoundly embedded in a phrase, its meaning determined and thoroughly coloured by the content of the context.

Let us take the second point first. Clearly, the word is understood contextually rather than lexically when the language exists at a low level of differentiation. We have seen, however, that no area of language save the purely scientific works entirely in fully differentiated terms. Consequently, we most usually treat words as if they were indications to be clarified and interpreted by reference to their contexts. One has only to consider the word 'elemental' in vacuo, and then to observe its use in the above quoted passage, to see this process at work. We may therefore agree that poetry, in directing our attention to the way in which the word's significance is a product of its context, reveals a basic characteristic of our habitual use of language.

Let us take an example of holophrasis. Consider the difference

[1] ibid., p. 183.

between the significances of the word 'blood' in the following four statements:

1. His blood ran cold at the sight.
2. He decided to volunteer as a blood donor.
3. He gave his life's blood for his country.
4. There was bad blood between them.

Although the 'import' of statements 2 and 3 may be the same, the emotive effect of the words 'life' and 'country' with their rich associative possibilities affects the associative strength of the word 'blood', while the intellectual, determinate quality of the words 'donor' and 'decided' prevents it from achieving any strength on the irrational intuitive level. Again, in number 1, the word is given an association of terror because it is in a context which describes an unnatural and therefore alarming occurrence. Thus its connections with ideas of murder, sacrifice, dread, and pain are aroused, while in number 4 the sentence contrives to see blood in terms of a relationship between people, and in terms of the life fluid, so that the associations of blood, as a word denoting tribe or race, come into play, as do associations of physical health or disease.

It can be seen from this, perhaps extreme, example that a word with a big associative fringe can alter its essential meaning to such an extent in different contexts that not only the emotional effect, but the actual concept, changes. One cannot imagine the 'blood' of sentence 3 running cold, or the blood of sentence 1 applying to sentence 2. They are not synonymous though they are the same word. Indeed, one cannot perceive the existence of one basic concept capable of being drastically affected by the context in which it is placed, unless one so phrases the concept that it satisfies Werner's definition of holophrasis. Thus the context is responsible more for the selection of applicable meaning from a wide range of possibilities, than for the enriching and overloading of one original meaning with other meanings and associations. We may suspect, therefore, that the reader or speaker may habitually create his own meanings for given words according to their contexts; he may, in reading or writing a word, use the general import of a sentence in which that word appears and also the associative power of adjacent words, in order to either interpret or engineer the appropriate meaning and emotional 'tone'. We may even postulate that man, in using words, does not accept a single meaning as basic and allow it to be enriched by its context, but accepts a holophrastic meaning and, by selection, fits it into the larger unit of language. I. A. Richards, concentrating upon the way in which the poem can define meanings, rather than upon the way in which it can present multiplicity of meaning, pointed out in his *Principles of Literary Criticism*:[1]

> A single word by itself, let us say 'night', will raise almost as many different thoughts and feelings as there are persons who hear it. The range of variety with a single word is very little restricted. But put it into a sentence and the variation is narrowed; put it into the context of a whole passage, and it is still further fixed; and let it occur in such an intricate whole as a poem and the responses of competent readers may have a similarity which only its occurrence in such a whole can secure.

Richards' statement must be qualified by experience. All readers of poetry know that in some instances the single word may be not limited but enlarged in meaning by the poem in which it appears so that, at the poem's conclusion, the word may indeed 'raise almost as many different thoughts and feelings as there are persons who hear it' and we might here instance the use Yeats made of the coat upon a coat-hanger as well as the Xanadu of *Kubla Khan* and images in many other poems. Nevertheless we have now reached the point where we can look back upon the poet's 'spatial' attitude to words and recognize it as being in no way abnormal; it is rather an intense awareness of the nature of the normal interpretative process of understanding language. We can indeed suggest that the poem, by making us aware of the associative and holophrastic characteristics of language, is more in accordance with the observable facts, than the piece of writing which makes precise use of the lexical system.

When one decides that a theory is in accordance with the observable facts one must be careful to indicate the area in which the facts have been observed. We cannot say that poetry, because of its accurate reflection of man's relationship to language, is more true than any non-poetic piece of writing, unless that piece of writing is attempting to portray something of man's mental and linguistic processes by presenting those processes in action, rather than by relating them to other processes by the use of the lexical system. Truth is also a word, and subject to the influences we have indicated. Faced with the statement that such a thing is true, we must always ask, 'True in what way, and True to what?' Bearing this in mind, let us tackle the basic problem of how man reaches the point of being able to attach any meaning at all to words. Obviously

[1] *Principles of Literary Criticism*, Routledge and Kegan Paul, 1924, pp. 9–10.

words are not meaningful only when found in the context of larger linguistic units. The lexicon is not a complete sham. What is the process of learning and recognizing words ?

First of all the child makes noises by instinct. Yells of pain or hunger are at first almost indistinguishable from each other, and are reflex actions. Very soon indeed, however, the child discovers that it is possible to use his voice in a more satisfactory fashion. By constant experimentation he discovers a whole range of sound, as he discovers a whole range of movements. At first these sounds are made, apart from hunger, anger, or pain cries, entirely experimentally, but after a time he notices that certain types of sound have certain results. The sound 'da-da' has something to do with those larger beings who feed him, wash him, clothe him, cuddle him, and control him. Anything that appears to require propitiation, affection, thus receives this sound. Gradually the 'portmanteau' quality of the noise decreases. 'Da-da' is used at the sight of any human being. Then it is used only to apply to male human beings. Finally it becomes a word meaning Father.

As time goes on more words are learnt, largely because the child has discovered the power of language. Make a certain sound and a certain object is pointed at, or profferred, or a certain action performed. We are not concerned at the moment with this early conviction about the nature of words, however, but we must return to it later. At present we must notice how the word 'da-da' develops and how it gathers meanings. Before the child is very old the word 'Dada' or 'Father' or 'Daddy' or 'Papa' has achieved considerable associative power, and has become a 'portmanteau' word. Analysis of it would show that it would be likely to arouse ideas of strength, frequent absence, tobacco smell, trousers, kissing mother, disinclination to wash up, clumsy tenderness, and a hundred other characteristics of the particular father concerned. At this point the word has achieved a kind of holophrasis because of continual usage in different contexts. The same argument applies to the word learnt from the dictionary, a word which has been first understood in terms of other words used by the lexicographer.

As time proceeds usage causes associative accretions, and an honest self-examiner would find himself defining the word in many ways that no dictionary would ever accept, were he to attempt a full description of the word's meanings and associations. All this is, of course, common knowledge, but worth repeating in order to show that no word is ever first understood as a phenomenon inseparable from other phenomena, and that even the lexicon provides some kind of associative fringe once it is consulted, while words like 'Dada', 'Mama', 'nasty', 'good', and so forth, cannot avoid having considerable associative power.

It could be maintained that the associative power of words remains unperceived in normal conversation, unless it is deliberately emphasized, and that when we read or hear a word we simply notice a central and obvious significance and are aware of no nuances or ambiguities whatsoever. Consequently, in talking of poetry as reflecting a characteristic of man's relationship to language, we are guilty of an exaggeration. We should have said 'a characteristic of man's relationship to language during childhood, and at moments of abnormal sensitivity'. After all, when someone says, 'I am going to the fish shop', we do not think of the sea or of swimming or trawlers. In order to answer this objection we must turn again to developmental psychology.

Heinz Werner, by means of several experiments, has shown that our understanding of a given word is a process of microgenesis, or 'unfolding'.[1] He suggests, indeed, that 'any human activity such as perceiving, thinking, acting, etc. is an unfolding process, and this unfolding or "microgenesis" occurs in developmental sequence'. By a study of aphasic patients, as well as normal people, he discovered that when presented with a word we first of all perceive a 'sphere of meaning', and then proceed to guide ourselves towards a specific meaning.

If a word is flashed upon a screen for one-fiftieth of a second, and an observer is asked to say what the word was, we find that only a vague general impression of the word's significance can be stated. This general impression is invariably in terms of qualities which we would associate with the word. For example, the first impression of one person presented with the phrase 'heulender Lärm' (howling noise) was as follows: 'The first pattern of letters produced for me the picture of something in sweeping motion, such as clouds of dust stirred up and driven by high winds through narrow streets.' Another person presented with the three words 'friedlich traurig gütig' (peaceful, sad, kind) said 'traurig—. Three words all "heavy", related to each other.' A second view produced the statement, 'traurig—ig—. Three adjectives . . . the whole rather "soft" and in a "minor key".' From such experiments Werner deduced that in recognizing words we first of all grasp their 'general dynamic, vectorial quality' and their 'atmosphere' before we follow the 'cues' provided by context or by the groups of sounds or letters, and achieve the

---

[1] Heinz Werner, 'Microgenesis and Aphasia', *Journal of Abnormal and Social Psychology*, 1956, 52, 347–53.

'correct' meaning. At the early stage, indeed, the word is recognized only as belonging to a certain *gestalt*, a certain area, and having certain qualities; if we accept his findings we must therefore agree that the concept 'fish' in the sentence, 'I am going to the fish shop', is selected from a host of associated possibilities as we speak or write it down. Admittedly this microgenetical process is usually so quick as to be unidentifiable as a process, though when one is tired or half asleep it is sometimes possible to feel it occurring.

It is clear, then, that the poet, in being aware of 'portmanteau' meaning is observing accurately, not only the associative power and general instability of language, but also the process of microgenesis and the way in which the recognition of spheres of meaning precedes the recognition of any specific and precise denotation. He is, indeed, by continually demanding from the reader a sensitivity to associative power, and an awareness of the way in which significances unfold themselves throughout the poem's length, forcing him into a recognition of the full complexity of the linguistic process.

TWO The Space Within

The poet, at the moment of writing, does not only feel that words have 'portmanteau meaning' and possess different degrees of focality, but also that each word, as he writes it or says it, is inextricably involved in his own sense of life. He participates in it the same way as a man participates in a friend to whom he is sympathetic, putting himself as much as is possible 'inside his skin'. It is an empathetic process. This feeling of participation is similar to the feeling of children and of many so-called primitive races, who are unable to conceive of anything as lacking the kind of life which they themselves possess. The stone, the tree, the rain, the hill, all exist, and are therefore alive. They live in a mythopoeic universe: there are no objects. This comes close to the belief of some modern thinkers that there is no perceived phenomenon which can exist apart from the action of perceiving. We are all part of what we say we see.

As O. S. Wauchope has written, 'The fact that there goes to the making of all reality something of the self for whom it *is* reality . . . appears in the Theory of Relativity; but professional philosophers have taken very little notice of the Theory of Relativity. As for the prediction-seeking laiety, some of that Theory's implications seem to them quite comical as "not standing to reason". And yet, a man has but to acknowledge that he is a self, and by implication he has allowed that there is a subjective factor in all his awareness and in all his intellectual operations; and then the notion of absolute objectivity, of events as in a fixed time-framework, or of number or matter or anything else of the not-self independently "existing", discovers to him its ultimate meaningless-ness.'[1] The process of perception is not as simple as we may sometimes think; the 'translation' of a collection of sense data into an 'object' is, most frequently, instantaneous, unconscious, and automatic. This translation has been described by Barfield in the following terms:

[1] O. S. Wauchope, *Deviation into Sense*, Faber and Faber, 1948, pp. 11–12.

18

On the assumption that the world whose existence is independent of our sensation and perception consists solely of 'particles', two operations are necessary (and whether they are successive or simultaneous is of no consequence), in order to produce the familiar world we know. First, the sense-organs must be related to the particles in such a way as to give rise to sensations; and secondly, those mere sensations must be combined and constructed by the percipient mind into the recognizable and nameable objects we call 'things'. It is this work of construction which will be here called *figuration*.[1]

This description of the process of figuration illustrates the essentially subjective quality of 'reality'. The construction must be made in order to 'fit in' with other constructions already made, and with deductions made from those constructions. Our beliefs condition our 'recognition' of a given object as a cross or a kettle. Our figuration, our making an object from the sense stimuli presented, is part of the 'reality' of that object.

The 'reality' we create, however, is complex, for we recognize 'things' in terms of their functions as well as their appearance. That is to say, we make suppositions about their functions in terms of our previous experience. If we are unable to do this we ask, 'What is it?' or even make mistakes, or what observers would call mistakes. We may call an ice-pick a dagger, a poncho a blanket, an antimacassar a table mat. If we are strangers to the culture in which we find ourselves we may become extremely perplexed; a nineteenth-century eskimo would almost certainly recognize glass as ice and then be unable to understand its relatively warm temperature, and there are countless instances of people in so-called primitive communities mistaking objects of use for objects of adornment. Sometimes these figurations appear extremely imaginative, and sometimes they are actually so. The child who knows full well that a basin is a basin will, nevertheless, call it and use it as a hat; he will call a dustbin lid a shield, a wooden spoon a spear. Sometimes he will grow angry if the reality of his figurations is denied; 'It's *not* an old log, it's my ship!!' he will say. While this is usually regarded as fantasizing, as playing, it is really also a perfectly usual use of the ordinary figuration process. The function, or possible function, of the object has qualified the process of recognition. The name, moreover, has created the object; the act of naming is an act of creation, as indeed it is regarded in many creation myths, and in the beliefs of many West African peoples.

Barfield points out that once the objects are 'made' and named, we

[1] Owen Barfield, *Saving the Appearances*, Faber and Faber, 1957, p. 24.

tend to 'treat them as independent of ourselves; to accept their "outness" as self-evidently given; and to speculate about or to investigate their relations *with each other*.'[1] For this kind of activity, he suggests the term, alpha-thinking. Of course, once alpha-thinking has resulted in a series of comparisons which enable objects of a given category to be individuated, the process of figuration may, in its unconscious assumptions, make use of this result; the immediate recognition by a botanist of a tree as an ash or oak is a case in point. Not all thinking is of this kind, however. The activity in which we are at present involved is neither figuration nor alpha-thinking—it is 'thinking about thinking' and this Barfield has chosen to call 'beta-thinking'.

With this armoury of terms available it becomes possible to see more clearly the difference between the poetic and the non-poetic attitude to phenomena. Anthropologists have pointed out that the primitive's participation in his personalized universe includes 'an awareness, which we no longer have, of an extra-sensory link between the percipient and the representations. This involves, not only that we think differently, but that the phenomena . . . themselves are different.'[2] This, of course, gave rise to initiation ceremonies, to the notion of Mana, of the life-force, and so on: it also made magic inevitable. If the subjective element is consistently recognized, then the imagined thing is as much a reality as the tangible. It exists, and its existence is not seriously different in kind. Therefore the 'name' creates the person. Therefore we cannot separate the name from the man—the one conjures up the other, truly presents the other. (One can see why certain primitive people keep their names a secret, only using substitute names, or nick-names, which of course, have not the same power.) Nor can we separate the part from the whole, the symbol from the symbolized.

All this, true of the primitive, is true of the poetic attitude. The poet, like the primitive, is keenly aware that we participate in phenomena not only as individuals but also as members of a given society and possessors of history. He will 'recognize' a dove, and in this recognition also be immediately aware of qualities, emotional and imaginative, and notions, from myth and history. Man, not only as a lone individual, but as a product of history and evolution, is involved in all the phenomena he perceives. It can be seen now that the poet's 'spatial' attitude is at one with his 'participant' attitude. The 'recognition' of the associative power

[1] Owen Barfield, op. cit., p. 24.
[2] ibid., p. 34.

of a word, the complex echoes and intimations it arouses, is as immediate, however, as the botanist's 'recognition' of the ash. Each perceives a patterned whole, and not a collection of parts, though each may be capable of explaining the details of the figuration process afterwards.

Once this is established it is easy to see why poetry has been considered anti-scientific. Science, as technology, deals in 'objects' set apart from the subjectivity of the individual observer, and the poet does not believe these objects to exist in the form technology supposes. It is also easy to see that the poet must feel complete understanding to be possible only in terms of an art form, which includes this element of human participation. Indeed, knowledge can only be complete knowledge if it is experienced by the total personality.

There is another aspect of knowledge, of understanding, which we must discuss if we are to get any closer to the nature and means of poetic understanding. In order to understand anything at all we must be able to perceive a pattern, a design. 'All comprehension', writes O. S. Wauchope, 'is comprehension of a pattern. If a thing is difficult to understand, that is because it is not easily seen as a pattern. Rhythmical and symmetrical things are different from others only in that they are easiest of all to comprehend as pattern, i.e. to comprehend.'[1]

Now, as I pointed out in an earlier essay,[2] the most striking thing about a poem is its pattern-quality. From the earliest times devices of rhythm, alliteration, and rhyme have ensured that, whatever else a poem does, it does present a pattern. I suggested in that earlier book that, as man understands and perceives entirely by making patterns, the poem by being so obviously a pattern presents him with an experience embodying a formal indication of the way in which all experience is perceived. Consequently the poem does not only present a pattern of some aspect of life, but also an experience of the nature of pattern itself. This aspect of artistic form has been well described by Wauchope.[3]

Pattern is the essential nature of all things, including works of art; but a work of art is different from other things in that the artist has worked to make it a thing with a pattern-nature so conspicuous that to contemplate it is an experience more of pattern than of thing. It is a thing with its intelligibility more to the fore than its thing-hood. It is a thing designed for us to understand not half but fully, it is a thing that can give us that rare experience. It is a

[1] O. S. Wauchope, op. cit., p. 19.
[2] Robin Skelton, *The Poetic Pattern*, Routledge and Kegan Paul, 1956.
[3] O. S. Wauchope, op. cit., p. 107.

whole of qualitative/quantitative parts—not a mere collection of parts, like six pennies in a row. Consequently, any part is the whole in miniature, and the whole is all reality in miniature. And there are hundreds of parts for emphasis; so that the beholder (or the listener, for this applies to works of art in any medium) becomes so pattern-saturated that his consciousness is filled more with the thing as pattern than with the thing as thing. And that *is* for him a strange third order of experience, at once joyous and sad, balanced as if life and death were for a few moments held separate before his gaze.

Such a moment of balance is mortal understanding at its most comprehensive . . .

Robert Frost's poem, *Design*,[1] begins with the presentation of a particular pattern and ends with questions about design itself.

Design

I found a dimpled spider, fat and white,
On a white heal-all, holding up a moth
Like a white piece of rigid satin cloth—
Assorted characters of death and blight
Mixed ready to begin the morning right,
Like the ingredients of a witches' broth—
A snow-drop spider, a flower like froth,
And dead wings carried like a paper kite.

What had that flower to do with being white,
The wayside blue and innocent heal-all?
What brought the kindred spider to that height,
Then steered the white moth thither in the night?
What but design of darkness to appall?—
If design govern in a thing so small.

Frost may well have begun his poem by noticing that there was a pattern in what he was seeing, and by perceiving its spatial, its 'portmanteau' quality. Frequently a poet begins his work with something less definite. He may start writing with only a sense of pattern in his mind—sometimes a rhythm, sometimes a tune, sometimes just the intuition that somehow or other a pattern in language is imminent. 'The order for the artist in his creative act is—pattern . . . thing.'[2] This pattern, however, cannot exist as a disembodied quality. It must be of something. It must have parts. And if it is to give to the poet who first perceives it,

---

[1] *The Complete Poems of Robert Frost*, Jonathan Cape, 1951, p. 330.
[2] O. S. Wauchope, op. cit., p. 108.

and the reader who perceives it later, that sense of an escape from time, a momentary complete understanding by the total personality of the nature of existence, the pattern must, in its parts, correspond to the parts involved in the act of human perception itself. This is not only to say that the elements of thought, emotion, feeling, intuition, must be clearly present, but also that its form must correspond to man's situation in time and space. There must be, obviously, variations in dimension, scale, and focality, as we have already mentioned. There must be the element of sequence, of movement forward, as well as the element of extension in space. There must be tension, kinesis, unity, and fragmentation. The poem must exist in such a way as to be, effectively, a linguistic analogue of perceiving man. It differs from analogues only in that it is not set apart from that which it parallels, but is an implement for the original to recognize itself. A mirror, we might say, constantly hoping to reflect face-to-face, and no longer darkly.

Poetry is not made of attitudes and ambitions, however, but of words, and in order to understand its modus operandi we must know something about the development of words themselves. Language, it is widely believed, began as a series of indicative sounds. Whether these sounds gained their value as indications from mimicking the noises associated with the objects indicated, or the noises that instinctively occurred on man's being faced with a certain physical or emotional environment, does not greatly matter to us at present. These sounds were widely manipulatable. A given sound could be used to indicate a wide number of phenomena. No sense of generalization was involved however. Noise X could indicate a mountain, a breast, a molehill, a buffalo, a mammoth, and a sensation of well-being. The reason behind this range was never considered. The factor of rounded shape common to the physical features and the animals, as well as to the full stomach which was naturally associated with well-being, would never be isolated, for to isolate this factor would be Beta-thinking, a late development in mankind.

As time progressed, however, these 'portmanteau words' became split up, as, by a process of at first clumsy alpha-thinking, the relationships between phenomena and their differences were clearly seen, and then incorporated unconsciously in the process of figuration. Thus, instead of the noise X to which we have already referred we would have word Y (indicating mountain, breast, molehill, well-being) and word Z indicating buffalo and mammoth. Later alpha-thinking made differentiation proceed further until language arrived at the position of including separate and distinct words for many particular phenomena. This stage of the development of language can be noticed today in primitive communities. Bertil Weman points out that 'in primitive languages there is a lack of denominations, e.g. of the species of cow, fox, squirrel, etc., but abundance of specific denominations of every sort of cow, fox, etc. (red cow, white cow, etc.).'[1] The next stage of development, linguistically, is obviously the beginnings of beta-thinking. Once the primitive begins to examine his figurations and alpha-thinking with the question, 'In what way are these phenomena similar; in what way can I group these under headings, give family or tribal names', he is indulging in beta-thinking of a simple kind, for he is not really examining the relationships between objects, as such, but the relationship between objects and the perceiving mind. He is 'thinking about thinking'. Thus, the generalization is the product of a much later linguistic attitude than the portmanteau word, and the two are not to be confused.

The difference between the generalization and the portmanteau word is important. The portmanteau word indicates both emotional states and physical objects. There is no idea of separating the two, for participation in the object is naturally accepted. A generalization, however, groups phenomena together under the heading of a named quality. And the name, once uttered, gives rise to a series of possible particulars in the mind, the context determining which particular is intended or relevant. We can still see traces of this early kind of generalization in Arabic where tent and camel are both referred to by the same word. The fully developed generalization or category word, however, does not give rise to the sensation of particulars to the same degree. If we were to generalize our word X we might get a word meaning 'that which is rounded or humped'. That is one common factor. Word Y might produce 'that which is rounded or humped' again, while word Z would give us 'that which is rounded and humped and has four legs'. These still have the possibility of arousing in the hearer's mind a series of possible particulars, but something is beginning to disappear. What is disappearing is very clear, if we take a leap into the future, and refer to the word 'mammal'. This word pretends to be objective. It has not the immediate sense of personal involvement to be found in X, and covers so wide a field as to make the immediate feeling of possible particulars unlikely. Indeed, because we cannot feel intensely towards anything but

[1] Bertil Weman, *Old English Semantic Analysis and Theory*, Lund. A. B. Ph., Linstedts Univ. Bokhandel, 1933, p. 10.

a particular as soon as the process of generalization becomes at all developed, the sense of participation begins to disappear. It is possibly true to say that a language which contains the words 'category', 'generalization', and 'group', is a language which has moved away from participation to a very great extent.

And yet no language can be completely non-participant. It is all a matter of degree. And language works, not in isolated words, but by means of linguistic patterns. Here again, a difference between primitive and sophisticated language appears. The primitive portmanteau word is only vaguely indicative unless it is in a sentence; the sentence invariably involves a personal expression, a personal manipulation of data; thus the subjective nature of perception is implied in every group of portmanteau words. The portmanteau word itself is, indeed by its very nature, indicative of a personal involvement. There is no pretence that the phenomena are to be regarded as apart from the perceiver. Roman Jacobson, in his essay, 'Linguistics and Poetics', draws attention to another way in which linguistic communication involves participation. He writes:[1]

> A former actor of Stanislavskij's Moscow Theater told me how at his audition he was asked by the famous director to make forty different messages from the phrase *Segodnja večerom* 'This evening', by diversifying its expressive tint. He made a list of some forty emotional situations, then emitted the given phrase in accordance with each of these situations, which his audience had to recognize only from the changes in the sound shape of the same two words. For our research work in the description and analysis of contemporary Standard Russian (under the auspices of the Rockefeller Foundation) this actor was asked to repeat Stanislavskij's test. He wrote down some fifty situations framing the same elliptic sentence and made of it fifty corresponding messages for a tape record. Most of the messages were correctly and circumstantially decoded by Moscovite listeners.

The point here is that words and phrases are all, to a degree, capable of multiple meaning, and that the tone of voice with which a word or phrase is spoken, and the interpretation of that tone of voice by the listener, play a considerable part in the process of communication. We do not need Jacobson to prove this to us if we only pause for a moment to think of how many different and meaningful inflexions can be given the word 'Hello' or how we can, in conversation, express disgust, affection,

[1] Roman Jacobson, 'Linguistics and Poetics' in Richard and Fernand De George, *The Structuralists from Marx to Lévi-Strauss*, Anchor Books, 1972, p. 91.

ill-temper, doubt, mockery, and delight by means of our tone of voice. Words are indeed even more semantically unstable when spoken than when written. It is not merely that an 'emotional' meaning may be given a statement by a tone of voice, but that the 'emotional' meaning will inevitably direct the attention of the listener to one or more of the meanings available. Thus if we say of a woman, 'She is very beautiful', we can, by emphasizing the word 'very', suggest that she is indeed superlatively attractive, while by emphasizing the word 'beautiful' we can easily imply that, while she is beautiful, there is not much else to her. If we make the tone interrogative we are altering the meaning yet again, and in all cases we are bringing into our statement some of the associations we have surrounding the word beautiful, such as the old saw that 'Beauty is only skin deep', the notion that 'Handsome is as handsome does', and even Keats' 'A thing of beauty is a joy for ever'.

It is obvious that poetry takes this aspect of semantic stability into account, for one of the functions of regular metre and rhythm is to control the emphases given the words. Over-emphasis of a word in a line will wreck the speech tune as effectively as under-emphasis. Moreover the well-made verse controls the speed with which the line is spoken, and this controls the tone of the voice also. One cannot gabble 'Dark, Dark, Dark amid the blaze of noon' and one cannot, without destroying the line, over-emphasize the words 'blaze' and 'noon' at the expense of the repeated word 'dark'. Poetry, because it is highly patterned, controls a great deal of the semantic instability of language, even while obliging us to recognize it. Sometimes, indeed, a poem can even indicate that it is the pattern, the apprehension of pattern which is the important matter, rather than the perception of the elements in the pattern. Wallace Stevens in his *Thirteen Ways of Looking at a Blackbird* gives us thirteen patterns in which the blackbird appears, each time having a somewhat different meaning, or rather significance, to the perceiver. In this way he shows how the perceiver 'creates' his perception, as well as how one single, very simple image can be so deployed as to imply many different perceptions. Indeed, the blackbird in the poem could be replaced by almost any other simple visual image though in order to avoid total absurdity it would have to be a living creature native to New England or some of the rest of the words would have to be altered as well. On the other hand it would, in the case of this particular poem, be perfectly possible to rewrite almost the whole thing with a different set of images and come up with much the same over-all message. This is, perhaps, an experiment worth trying. Here as a kind of interlude is Wallace Stevens' *Thirteen Ways of Looking at a Blackbird*[1] alongside a poem of my own in imitation of it.

Thirteen Ways of Looking at a Blackbird

I

Among twenty snowy mountains,
The only moving thing
Was the eye of the blackbird.

II

I was of three minds,
Like a tree
In which there are three blackbirds.

III

The blackbird whirled in the autumn winds.
It was a small part of the pantomime.

IV

A man and a woman
Are one.
A man and a woman and a blackbird
Are one.

V

I do not know which to prefer,
The beauty of inflections
Or the beauty of innuendoes,
The blackbird whistling
Or just after.

VI

Icicles filled the long window
With barbaric glass.
The shadow of the blackbird
Crossed it, to and fro.
The mood
Traced in the shadow
An indecipherable cause.

[1] Wallace Stevens, *Collected Poems*, Faber and Faber, 1955, p. 92.

VII

O thin men of Haddam,
Why do you imagine golden birds?
Do you not see how the blackbird
Walks around the feet
Of the women about you?

VIII

I know noble accents
And lucid, inescapable rhythms;
But I know, too,
That the blackbird is involved
In what I know.

IX

When the blackbird flew out of sight,
It marked the edge
Of one of many circles.

X

At the sight of blackbirds
Flying in a green light,
Even the bawds of euphony
Would cry out sharply.

XI

He rode over Connecticut
In a glass coach.
Once, a fear pierced him,
In that he mistook
The shadow of his equipage
For blackbirds.

XII

The river is moving.
The blackbird must be flying.

XIII

It was evening all afternoon.
It was snowing
And it was going to snow.
The blackbird sat
In the cedar-limbs.

Thirteen Ways of Looking at a Black Mackintosh

i

Among scores of hurrying women
The only disturbing thing
Was the gleam of her black mackintosh.

ii

I was of three minds
Like a closet
In which there are three black mackintoshes.

iii

The black mackintosh glistened among the daffodils.
It was one clue to the bacchanal.

iv

A man with a woman
Is glad.
A man with a woman in a black mackintosh
Is glad.

v

I do not know which to prefer,
The moment of acceptance
Or the moment of hesitation,
The black mackintosh unbuttoning
Or a little earlier.

vi

Late sunlight barred the lawns
With shadows of trees.
The liberty of her black mackintosh
Crossed them, to and fro.
The sun
Lit from its movements
The primal cause.

vii

O sad men of America
Why do you dream of white evening gowns?
Do you not see how the black mackintosh
Glints winking creases
Above her rump?

viii

I know heroic frescoes
And vivid exuberant paintings;
But I know, too,
That the black mackintosh is a part
Of all I know.

ix

When the black mackintosh turned the corner
It marked the limit
Of all our revelations.

x

At the sight of a black mackintosh
Glistering in wet lamplight
Even the pillars of morality
Would shake softly.

xi

He bought a house in Rhode Island
With a Four-poster bed.
Once, a dream woke him
For it mistook
The shadows of his curtains
For black mackintoshes.

xii

Youth is over.
The black mackintosh hangs empty.

xiii

It was winter all summer long.
It was raining
And it was going to rain.
The black mackintosh shone
On her moving limbs.

Whatever else emerges from this perhaps not altogether serious interlude it is clear that both poems insist upon the subjective nature of perception, and indicate the semantic instability of language, the multiple possibilities of a single word or image. This insistence may not irritate poets and lovers of poetry, but it may well irritate others who base their lives and communications upon the supposition that words are stable in meaning, and that these meanings cannot be changed by anything but an act of God, or possibly of the Académie Française and the editors of the *Oxford English Dictionary*. A pejorative remark often heard today is that so-and-so's statement is 'highly subjective'; 'objectivity' is, we gather, to be praised. Poetry, however, must deal in the 'subjective' for if no sense of human participation is involved, if the linear is not at least occasionally mastered by the spatial perception, no-one will call the work poetry at all. Language today is often praised as being 'accurate' if it proceeds by way of narrow definitions and a developing series of differentiations. Epistemology depends upon this as much as does technology. Poetry, however, operates not only in terms of focality (which doubts both the possibility and value of accurate delimitation of meaning) but also in terms of patterns of perception that are held together in unity only by the presence of one frequently eccentric perceiver. The poet insists upon our participation in language; the grammarian, technologist, and logician demand that we subject ourselves to it.

THREE Metaphor and Emotion

The tension which exists between the language envisaged by the grammarian and that used by the poet is especially obvious today, for many twentieth-century poets have broken the 'rules' of syntax, scorned 'proper usage' and 'accepted' spelling, and denied the authority of the lexicographers. Every time a poem uses a verb as a noun, and vice-versa, or flagrantly offends good taste by its use of emphatic vulgarities, it challenges the validity of that conventional attitude which assumes the fixed positioning of each word in a grammatical and social scheme. In contrast to the implication of the lexicographer that language is a defined system of relationships based upon objective criteria, poetry asserts that each word exists as that which its context, affecting and altering a primary meaning and connotative complex, determines. It denies, by implication, the validity of the dictionary, and derides the notion of 'correct' usage.

An obvious instance of this is e. e. cummings' poem *anyone lived in a pretty how town*, in which the parts of speech are deliberately teased and tricked into performing new duties.[1]

> anyone lived in a pretty how town
> (with up so floating many bells down)
> spring summer autumn winter
> he sang his didn't he danced his did.
>
> Women and men (both little and small)
> cared for anyone not at all
> they sowed their isn't they reaped their same
> sun moon stars rain
>
> children guessed (but only a few
> and down they forgot as up they grew
> autumn winter spring summer)
> that noone loved him more by more

[1] e. e. cummings, *Complete Poems 1936–1962*, MacGibbon and Kee, 1968, Vol. II, p. 515.

when by now and tree by leaf
she laughed his joy she cried his grief
bird by snow and stir by still
anyone's any was all to her

someones married their everyones
laughed their cryings and did their dance
(sleep wake hope and then) they
said their nevers they slept their dream

stars rain sun moon
(and only the snow can begin to explain
how children are apt to forget to remember
with up so floating many bells down)

one day anyone died i guess
(and noone stooped to kiss his face)
busy folk buried them side by side
little by little and was by was

all by all and deep by deep
and more by more they dream their sleep
noone and anyone earth by april
wish by spirit and if by yes.

Women and men (both dong and ding)
summer autumn winter spring
reaped their sowing and went their came
sun moon stars rain

This may be an extreme instance, but only because the whole of the poem is based upon a game with language. Other instances which occur within poems that are less completely anti-grammatical are easy to find. The non-sentence is frequent, as is the lack of punctuation.

To Carthage then I came

Burning burning burning burning
O Lord Thou pluckest me out
O Lord Thou pluckest

burning

(T. S. ELIOT, *The Waste Land*)[1]

[1] T. S. Eliot, *Collected Poems 1909–1962*, Faber and Faber, 1963, p. 74.

Accepted meanings are wrenched by new contexts

> Huge is the sun of amethysts and rubies,
> And in the purple perfumes of the polar sun
> And homeless cold they wander
> <div align="right">(EDITH SITWELL, <i>The Song of the Cold</i>)[1]</div>

In spite of the activities of such inventive poets as these, the dictionary is, for many people, an incontrovertible authority. Yet a dictionary definition, when examined, soon reveals its arbitrary nature. This definition is invariably in terms of relationships (as is necessary) but only of relationship to a limited selection of other words, which selection has been made by regarding words as objects which can be grouped together according to their common characteristics. Thus the dictionary can define a tree as a vegetable growth, but not as an affecting personality. Yet trees, to ordinary people, can frequently have a disturbingly 'human' quality. Again, the dictionary will define a saucepan satisfactorily so long as one only sees a saucepan in a kitchen. If it is discovered on a rubbish heap in a garden next to a dahlia, it is quite another object. It is another object because of the subjective element in figuration. We can extend this farther if we realize that we are continually required to perceive relationships quite outside the scope of the lexicon. That white wall next to the blue door alters our whole idea of the nature of white, if we have been in the habit of deriving our idea of white from white paper on a brown table. How can we define white in terms of blue as well as in terms of brown ? How can we define a saucepan in terms of dahlias ? Or, recalling Wallace Stevens' poem, how can we define a blackbird in terms of an ice-covered window ? .

Relationship is our mode of perception and judgement. Figuration involves an automatic and unconscious establishment of relationship, just as much as alpha-thinking involves a conscious one. Definition is only a perception of relationship within a limited field that has been created as a consequence of other judgements of relationship within the social, grammatical, moral, syntactical, pseudo-logical system that man has created because he must work in terms of an accepted pattern, and have it as the basis for his action, even if he departs from it in casual conversation, or in instinctive activities.

It is, however, obvious that definition has its place. The dictionaries

---

[1] Edith Sitwell, <i>Collected Poems</i>, Macmillan, 1957, p. 292.

must not be burnt. It should be recognized that they are providing only primary meanings, however, and that these primary meanings are very much dependent upon a working system which has only a practical, and not an absolute, value.

It is the acceptance of the lexicon-attitude as true to the nature of experience that does the damage. Poetry attacks upon this front by presenting relationships which exist in experience, but not in the conventional language system of the lexicographer and grammarian. Almost any metaphor or simile from any poem can be used to illustrate this statement. The poem also, by emphasizing in its formal arrangement the quality of relationship as such, underlines the contrast. A brief glance at the nature of metaphor may help to explain this point further.

Metaphor can be regarded as being the middle term of three in a progress of imagery. The lowest, or most simple, use of imagery which involves the readers with the apprehension of a relationship between two or more objects is a simile, which the beta-thinking grammar book describes as 'A comparison involving the use of the words like or as'. Let us take 'He sang like a star' as being an appropriately irrational example. Here there is a presentation of separation. The irrationality of the relationship, however, forces us to accept the fact that it exists, not upon the objective, but upon the subjective plane. It is not a technological statement. Participation is involved at the very beginning. The language-system has been distorted in order to provide a verbal equivalent for a human experience having some emotional value. The star and the man may be compared but are still distinct from one another. The reference is 'outward' from the subject of the statement, the man, to another area of feeling or experience, and this reference outward is used solely to illuminate our understanding of the subject, as in such lines as

Like apples they fell off at one windfall, all,

(OSCAR WILLIAMS, *The Mirage*)[1]

The mirrored lights like sunken swords
　Glimmer and shake

(SARA TEASDALE, *Spring Night*)[2]

. . . night approaching like the entrance of a tunnel

(JEAN GARRIGUE, *Forest*)[3]

[1] In Oscar Williams (ed.), *A Little Treasury of Modern Poetry*, Routledge and Kegan Paul, 1947, pp. 335–6.
[2] ibid., pp. 322–3.　　　[3] ibid., pp. 252–3.

In these three examples it is easy to see that the two things compared are, indeed, similar in important and obvious respects. In other similes this is not the case, as in

> My heart is like a singing bird . . .
> My love is like a red red rose . . .

Here we have to make an effort to suspend our disbelief; we are forced to trust the poem, if we are to continue reading. Conflicts of this kind are more common in metaphors than in similes, and they are particularly frequent in the work of the so-called metaphysical poets. There are many kinds of conflict. Sometimes the difficulty of immediate acceptance lies in the differing scale of the subjects compared as in Donne's *The Good-Morrow*.[1]

> My face in thine eye, thine in mine appeares,
> And true plaine hearts doe in the faces rest,
> Where can we finde two better hemispheares
> Without sharpe North, without declining West?

Sometimes there appears to be a conflict in terms of the emotional tone as in George Barker's *Dog, Dog in my Manger*.[2]

> O my joy has jaws that seize in fangs

Here one word (joy) has associations and implications so different from those normally perceived for the accompanying words (jaw, fangs) that the line appears to have unified, by means of syntax, mutually exclusive notions. Metaphor, of course, always presents unity rather than separation—'an implied comparison', says the grammar, rather feebly. If we change our simile, 'He sang like a star', into metaphor we could get 'He was a singing star' which, although it presents the same meaning as the simile, unifies the two compared things and makes them one identity. The apprehension is of man *as* star, and consequently of star *as* man; participation has reached the stage of ascribing personality to the 'object'. The statement is a mythopoeic one, and implies that there is a life-force common to both object and subject. This statement is also

---

[1] John T. Shawcross (ed.), *The Complete Poetry of John Donne*, Anchor Books, 1967, p. 89.

[2] Oscar Williams (ed.), op. cit., p. 263.

capable of being developed without the use of intrusive conjunctions in a much more effective fashion than is the simile. The simile might be extended to read, 'He sang like a star that flared before it fell'. Here the act of flaring and falling only illuminates the act of singing, while, by omitting the verb which still separates the man from the star in our metaphor, and extending the metaphor, we can achieve, 'He was a singing star that flared before it fell', which makes it possible to regard the activities of flaring and falling as part of the activities of the man, as singer, or as anything else, while still indicating something about the singing. There are the beginnings of a rich ambiguity here. If we omit the verb, which still in this example separates the man from the star, we can achieve a still closer degree of identity with 'He, a singing star, flared out before he fell'. It is at this point that awareness of ambiguity begins to become awareness of focality. The statement, initially a rather pretty comparison, has now taken on a good deal of associative power. We are moved, consciously or unconsciously, by the image of the star itself, for that image, being completely fused with the image of man, has become independent of any merely comparative intention. The statement is one about a star as much as it is one about a man, only the star is mythopoeically treated, given vital force, so that our minds, reflecting on it, tend to enter the territory of myth. Comets and Christmasses attend us. There is an atmosphere of intense significance. We might say with Calpurnia,

> When beggars die there are no comets seen;
> The Heavens themselves blaze forth the death of princes

We are indeed on the verge of apprehending the Poetic Symbol (or would be, were not the illustration I have chosen an admirable example of semantic instability. Nowadays a 'singing star' has lost all its force as a phrase, indicating merely a popular entertainer). The word Symbol has been used so often that I suppose that I must repeat my own view of its nature for the purposes of this argument. The symbol is an archetypal image which has as its meaning the sum of all its associations and implications, and which is not limited in its power by any arbitrary comparison or any purely cerebral qualification. It has total focality. To have this effect it must be in a position of independence in the poem or linguistic structure. It must exist in its own right. As an example, we might consider the figure of the Ancient Mariner in Coleridge's poem. No matter what associations he brings to our mind, they all tend to apply; Wandering Jew, Judas, Ishmael, Pilate, Flying Dutchman, Murderer, Sinner against the Holy Ghost, Pilgrim, and so on. One example of a poem which is completely symbolist is Edwin Muir's *The Combat*. Whatever associations come to our minds concerning the two beasts appear to be relevant. Is the battle between the Aristocracy and the Proletariat, between Pride and Guilt, between Evil and Good? It is, I think, all of these and many more.[1]

It was not meant for human eyes,
That combat on the shabby patch
Of clods and trampled turf that lies
Somewhere beneath the sodden skies
For eye of toad or adder to catch.

And having seen it I accuse
The crested animal in his pride,
Arrayed in all the royal hues
Which hide the claws he well can use
To tear the heart out of the side.

Body of leopard, eagle's head
And whetted beak, and lion's mane,
And frost-grey hedge of feathers spread
Behind—he seemed of all things bred.
I shall not see his like again.

As for his enemy, there came in
A soft round beast as brown as clay;
All rent and patched his wretched skin;
A battered bag he might have been,
Some old used thing to throw away.

Yet he awaited face to face
The furious beast and the swift attack.
Soon over and done. That was no place
Or time for chivalry or for grace.
The fury had him on his back.

And two small paws like hands flew out
To right and left as the trees stood by.
One would have said beyond a doubt
This was the very end of the bout,
But that the creature would not die.

[1] Edwin Muir, *Collected Poems*, Faber and Faber, 1963, pp. 179–80.

For ere the death-stroke he was gone,
Writhed, whirled, huddled into his den,
Safe somehow there. The fight was done,
And he had lost who had all but won.
But oh his deadly fury then.

A while the place lay blank, forlorn,
Drowsing as in relief from pain.
The cricket chirped, the grating thorn
Stirred, and a little sound was born.
The champions took their posts again.

And all began. The stealthy paw
Slashed out and in. Could nothing save
These rags and tatters from the claw?
Nothing. And yet I never saw
A beast so helpless and so brave.

And now, while the trees stand watching, still
The unequal battle rages there.
The killing beast that cannot kill
Swells and swells in his fury till
You'd almost think it was despair.

This poem illustrates an extreme. Symbolism of this absolute kind is not present in all poetry, whereas almost all poetry contains metaphor; certainly it is hard to regard metaphor as being less than central to poetic language. We can see now that its usage involves almost all the attitudes so far described. It has the power to have symbolic value, multiple meaning, multiple association, and focality while remaining ostensibly tied to the function of comparison. It therefore can present not merely separation, in that comparison is involved, but also fusion of the two or more separate matters involved into a unity. It is always, to some extent, a portmanteau phrase. It regards all phenomena as being so closely related that they can be identified with each other; it accepts the fundamental equality and unity of all things. The star is the man is the singing: all are animate; each is as real as the other two, all having the same type of existence. It involves the reader, too, in an immediate sense of participation. All things are subjects. All things, too, are different concrete instances of the presence of life. It is because the poet naturally perceives life in this fashion that metaphor is, to him, an inevitable way of speech. Northrop Frye has argued this most cogently.[1]

> ... And as in the imaginative view all things are within the life of a single eternal and infinite God-Man, all aspects, forms or images of that body are identical. This is a view of things which can only be expressed poetically, through metaphor. The metaphor, in its radical form, is a statement of identification: the hero is a lion; this is that; A is B. When the hero is metaphorically a lion he remains a hero and the lion remains a lion. Hence a world where everything is identical with everything else is not a world of monotonous uniformity, as a world where everything was *like* everything else would be. In the imaginative world everything is one in essence, but infinitely varied in identity, as Blake remarks in a note on Swedenborg.

We have already seen that the poet's way of perception is no different from the normal; his attitude towards his perception differs only in that he forces his language to correspond with it, rather than deny it. He exposes the subjective element to such an extent that his world is personalized. Metaphor is one of the means by which this is achieved. Shakespeare provides us with examples, not only of alpha-thinking, but also of beta-thinking presented in such a way that participation is inevitable.

> So sharp are hungers teeth

> Clock-setter time

> My state being galled with my expense
> I seek to heal it only by his wealth

This simple personification is only one method, of course. There are many others. All of them, however, administer a shock to the reader by forcing him to abandon logic. When Shakespeare refers to Antony as 'The triple pillar of the world transformed into a strumpet's fool', we know full well that Antony is not, in fact, a pillar. Yet, in order to read the line, we must perceive him as one. This activity causes us, at least while reading the play, to accept the validity of purely mental events. The imagined is as real as the actual. Once we have taken this step, we

---

[1] Northrop Frye, 'Notes for a Commentary on *Milton*', in *The Divine Vision, Studies in the Poetry and Art of William Blake*, ed. Vivian de Sola Pinto, Gollancz, 1957, p. 107.

can accept statements like 'My heart is in the coffin there with Caesar' without batting an eyelid. In accepting such a statement as valid perception, we do not often realize the implications of our acceptance, however, and these implications are important.

First of all let us notice that this type of statement requires us to observe the holophrastic nature of language. We can only accept the statement that a man is a pillar if we realize that the word pillar has multiple meaning, or at least a series of valid associations. Ideas of strength, support, hardness, and durability must be associated with the notion of a 'pillar' for us to perceive, first, that the statement implies qualities of authority, responsibility, and endurance in the man, and, secondly, that the transformation of the pillar to the strumpet's fool (associations here of laxity, irresponsibility, impulsiveness, moral weakness) is meaningful as a description of character. A further complexity is added to the phrase by the ambiguity of the word fool, an ambiguity given it by the phallic association of 'pillar' and the sexual significance of 'strumpet': 'fool' conveys, indeed, at once the notion of a hired jester or clown and a phallus. The significance of this holophrastic element can easily be seen if we recall Werner's statement that 'holophrasis is a characteristic feature of slang, as well as of emotional language'. In this particular case, the holophrastic element looming so large on account of the abruptness and compass of the transition, we are forced to intuit the presence of very strong emotion, and perhaps even also suspect the presence of slang or euphemism, thus reinforcing our impression of the possible ambiguity of the word 'fool'. (We ought to recognize here, however, that it is not impossible that the printer transformed the word 'tool' to 'fool', and that Enobarbus was intended, at this point, to appear to be more bawdy and less truly passionate than the accepted text implies. This does not, however, affect our argument.)

The emotional effect of holophrasis is extremely important to the understanding of the construction of poetry, for it works in two ways. Once we recognize a word as holophrastic we intuit the presence of emotion (provided that the context does not clearly imply a purely cerebral witticism, a contrived decoration). On the other hand, once we recognize a word as an expression of strong emotion we immediately (though not always consciously) assume it to be holophrastic, to carry a considerable weight of association and implication. Some of these words are recognized as emotional because they are ones which have an intimate connection with the emotional life of every human being in the area in which the language is spoken. A 'stock response' can be expected.

Sometimes the rhythm attaches weight to a word, and thus draws attention to its emotional possibilities, for the more 'breath' we give a word, the more important we suppose it to be, adopting unconsciously the view that the word has been given more 'mana'. We find this occurring in arguments. People raise their voices in order to put more power into their words—not so much to make listening easier, but to make the speaker's personal conviction more communicable, to establish his complete and total belief in the statement he is making. Thus, the more emphasis the rhythm places upon a word (supposing the poem to be a good one), the more quickly do we associate the word with the presence of a convinced and impassioned person. Once we sense this presence we intuit also the presence of an intellectual and emotional complex beneath the surface, and are then inclined to perceive a high degree of associative implication.

This technique is usually used in combination with the presentation, at another point in the poem, of a complex of meanings. If the statement is made, 'The wood was black as ink', we may, because of the very slight oddity of the expression, find ourselves grouping one or two unimportant associations round the word 'ink'. If we read, 'The wood was black as tigers', because we have to search for some common factor between blackness and tigers, we find ourselves examining the associations and implications of both words, thus recognizing holophrasis and intuiting emotion. The intensity of the emotion becomes greater if the statement reads, 'The wood was tiger-black', or 'The wood was a tiger', for then, in order to see anything but nonsense in the statement we have to find some way in which tigers and woods can be identified, can be seen as living in the same area, inhabiting the same *gestalt*, possessing the same essence. The amount of searching involved corresponds closely to the intensity of the emotion perceived, provided always that nonsense is not suspected, and that we recognize that each reader must, sooner or later, reach a point where he is unwilling to attempt the search, or unable to carry it out quickly enough for the words to have any immediate impact. When we do this we are, of course, retracing, for each word or phrase, the process of microgenesis which we discussed earlier. We are, indeed, admitting to ourselves the microgenetical nature of our perception of language.

We can see from this that the metaphorical use of language forces us to recognize emotion, and thus forces us to regard the poem as being the product of a person, with whom we must enter into a participant relationship, a sympathetic relationship that is only partly intellectual, if we are completely to understand and experience what is going on. We are forced to assent to the reality of the poem's (or poet's) experience because we recognize that experience as being a whole; it involves not only intellectual but also emotional and intuitive elements, each one of which contributes to and qualifies the remainder, so that in order to appreciate any part we must accept the complete thing. In his poem, *Hasbrouck and the Rose*, Phelps Putnam shows how the poet, Smollet Smith, is forced to accept Hasbrouck's experience of the mystical rose, not because of Hasbrouck's intellectual understanding of the symbol, but because the rose has become a part of Hasbrouck's whole life. If he accepts any part of Hasbrouck he must also accept the rest, however much it terrifies him.[1]

> Hasbrouck was there and so were Bill
> And Smollet Smith the poet, and Ames was there.
> After his thirteenth drink, the burning Smith,
> Raising his fourteenth trembling in the air,
> Said, 'Drink with me, Bill, drink up to the Rose.'
> But Hasbrouck laughed like old men in a myth,
> Inquiring, 'Smollet, are you drunk? What rose?'
> And Smollet said, 'I drunk? It may be so;
> Which comes from brooding on the flower, the flower
> I mean toward which mad hour by hour
> I travel brokenly; and I shall know,
> With Hermes and the alchemists—but, hell,
> What use is it talking that way to you?
> Hard-boiled, unbroken egg, what can you care
> For the enfolded passion of the Rose?'
> Then Hasbrouck's voice rang like an icy bell:

> 'Arcane romantic flower, meaning what?
> Do you know what it meant? Do I?
> We do not know.
> Unfolding pungent rose, the glowing bath
> Of ecstasy and clear forgetfulness;
> Closing and secret bud one might achieve
> By long debauchery—
> Except that I have eaten it, and so
> There is no call for further lunacy.

[1] Phelps Putnam, *The Five Seasons*, Scribners, 1931, p. 19.

In Springfield, Massachusetts, I devoured
The mystic, the improbable, the Rose.
For two nights and a day, rose and rosette,
And petal after petal and the heart,
I had my banquet by the beams
Of four electric stars which shone
Weakly into my room, for there,
Drowning their light and gleaming at my side,
Was the incarnate star
Whose body bore the stigma of the Rose.
And that is all I know about the flower;
I have eaten it—it has disappeared.
There is no Rose.'

Young Smollet Smith let fall his glass; he said
'Oh Jesus, Hasbrouck, am I drunk or dead?'

This poem reaches out into strange territories, but its general method, the way in which it moves from linear to spatial vision, and the way in which it permits the timeless symbol to intrude upon the commonplace, is typical not only of much poetry, but also of metaphor itself, for the strength of metaphor lies in its invariable denial of the reality of our usual notions of time and space. Let us look again at the statement, 'My heart is in the coffin there with Caesar'. As soon as we look at it a second time we notice that the time-space continuum is being distorted. Common sense tells that if the heart is in the coffin it cannot be in Antony, and yet it must be if he is speaking. Time and space are juggled even more extensively in a line like 'I am the enemy you killed, my friend', yet poetry is full of such visitations. The simplest metaphor, identifying man with lion, involves a denial of clock-time and of the restrictions of space. The world of poetry is like the world of dream in that phenomena normally regarded as separate in time and space are fused together. In the dream one can have a friend who is also a tree, and, somehow, the taste of the cocoa drunk before retiring. In a poem we can have a lecher who is also a wind lying quiet in a mine.

The bawdy wind that kisses all it meets
Is hushed within the hollow mine of earth.

(Othello V.2. 78–9)

We can have:

> Broad-fronted Caesar,
> When thou wast here above the ground, I was
> A morsel for a monarch; and great Pompey
> Would stand, and make his eyes grow in my brow;
> There would he anchor his aspect, and die
> With looking on his life.
>
> (Antony and Cleopatra I.5. 29–34)

We can have:

> Soft is the collied night, and cool
> These regions where the dreamers rule,
> As summer, in her rose and robe,
> Astride the horses of the globe,
> Drags, fighting, from the midnight sky,
> The mushroom at whose glance we die.
>
> (GEORGE BARKER, *Summer Song II*)[1]

This attitude to phenomena is also an attitude towards the nature of time. Only if the restrictions placed upon logical thinking by time and space are removed, and we can perceive a man of today whose 'beard wags in Egyptian Wind', can we read poetry. Only if we can accept every mental event as a present reality valid in itself can we adopt the metaphorical attitude towards phenomena. We are again back to the subjective nature of perception, but we are also faced with the problem of man's relationship to time, and, consequently, to the concepts of history, tradition, and evolution. Before we tackle this subject we may as well remind ourselves that the poet, at the time of composing, often feels himself to have escaped from time, that much poetry has been written about the 'timeless moment', and that, in attacking the language-system, poetry is also, inevitably, attacking that attitude towards time and space which makes the separation of object from object possible. Delimitation is a result of a particular time-sense. Definition is dependent upon a concept of space. If poetry is true to the nature of human perception, it must be true to the human experience of time and space, though not necessarily true to the formulations made about them. In section VII of his *Variations on a Time Theme*, Edwin Muir expressed poetry's passionate desire to escape the bondage of time in language

---

[1] George Barker, *Collected Poems 1930–1955*, Faber and Faber, 1957, p. 156.

which, because of its rapid succession of metaphors, asserts time's defeat by the poetic imagination.[1]

> Ransomed from darkness and released in Time,
> Caught, pinioned, blinded, sealed and cased in Time;
> Summoned, elected, armed and crowned by Time,
> Tried and condemned, stripped and disowned by Time;
> Suckled and weaned, plumped and full-fed by Time,
> Defrauded, starved, physicked and bled by Time;
> Buried alive and buried dead by Time:
>
> If there's no crack or chink, no escape from Time,
> No spasm, no murderous knife to rape from Time
> The pure and trackless day of liberty;
> If there's no power can burst the rock of Time,
> No Rescuer from the dungeon stock of Time,
> Nothing in earth or heaven to set us free:
> Imprisonment's for ever; we're the mock of Time,
> While lost and empty lies Eternity.

[1] Edwin Muir, op. cit., pp. 47–8.

FOUR Poetry and Space-time

It has been our contention so far that poetry, by its very structure, presents us with the real manner of our ordinary perception. We have found ourselves agreeing with John Dewey[1] that

> ... the esthetic is no intruder in experience from without ... it is the clarified and intensified development of traits that belong to every normally complete experience.

We have now reached a point where it becomes necessary to examine also the truth of another of Dewey's dicta. He suggested that

> Form, as it is present in the fine arts, is the art of making clear what is involved in the organization of space and time prefigured in every course of a developing life-experience.[2]

We are concerned, not with the fine arts as they are usually considered, but with poetry, and the word 'form' here may not mean exactly what we would have it to mean, but, in general, the statement is one we must examine.

Our first task must be to examine the nature of man's actual perception of space and time, as opposed to his workaday beliefs about them. We have already seen Barfield's attempt to show that the perceived world is, very largely, a construction by the percipient, and have deduced from this that there is no means of telling to what extent the constructs of different individuals faced with the same phenomena are similar. Let us now turn to the evidence of a neurologist, Sir Russell Brain, who has, in his book, *The Nature of Experience*,[3] provided some physiological

[1] John Dewey, *Art as Experience*, Allen and Unwin, 1934, p. 24.
[2] ibid., p. 24.
[3] Sir Russell Brain, *The Nature of Experience*, Oxford University Press, 1959, p. 23.

support for what has come to be known as the Sense-Datum Theory of Perception. Sir Russell points out that

> ... the facts of physics and physiology show that perception is the end-result of a series of physical events, the last of which, a state of activity of the brain of the percipient, differs so completely from the events occurring in the object perceived that the qualitative features of a percept can have no resemblance to the physical object which it represents. The perceptual world, therefore, if I may use the term to describe the whole realm of our perceptual experience, is a construct of the percipient's brain.

This means that the version of reality which we perceive must be regarded as being far from a mirror image of the reality 'outside' us, but more of a symbolic representation. It also means that the only difference between what we have loosely described as the perception of a mental event and the perception of reality is the percipient's notion that, since other people claim to be aware of the 'actuality', it is safe to infer that it has an independent existence of some kind. The percipient who makes this inference can bolster it up by observing that the system of 'actual' relationships he observes appears to correspond in the main with the system reported to him by other percipients: This is a white stone. That is a loud noise. And so forth. He has, however, no means of knowing whether the construct which he labels 'white stone' resembles the construct labelled 'white stone' by someone else. He knows only that, in his own system of symbolic constructs, this particular construct appears to have the same position relative to all other constructs as it has in the construct-system of his fellows. Not infrequently, however, there are disagreements. Where it is difficult for him to perceive the precise delimitations of the individual constructs of a group, he discovers that it is possible for his companions to disagree with him as to the nature of the actuality they are both observing. This happens frequently when he has to discuss fine shades of colour, or variations of sound, or taste. Fortunately for human communication, however, it is usually possible to bring so many modes of perception into play in the perceiving of a given actuality that a degree of cross-reference can identify the placing of that actuality in the construct-system with a good deal of apparent accuracy. Nevertheless one has only to blindfold three people and make them listen to a series of sounds, or handle a series of objects, to note how approximate agreement really is. Another interesting experiment consists of asking a group of people to write down what they see in their mind's eye immediately upon hearing a certain word. I have used the word 'tree' for this experiment on many occasions and in a group of twenty or so people have always found that the answers include at least three quite distinctly different types of tree as well as specific trees and such images as 'greenness', 'a cluster of leaves' and 'bare branches'. Another way to make people appreciate the way in which they themselves participate in their understanding of simple words is to ask such questions as 'What colour is a fence ?' and 'What colour is a door ?' In these instances the personal associations and experiences of the listeners contribute to the confusion.

Though our responses to individual words and images differ, and we frequently disagree about the exact description of a phenomenon, we usually assume that there is an actual world external to ourselves. Certainly our perceptual constructs appear to have counterparts in some external world for other people can refer to these counterparts in a meaningful way, and without any fundamental distortion of their characteristics. This is true if all the percipients are members of the same culture. If the cultures differ, as we have already said, the constructs can differ quite remarkably. A primitive tribesman's perception of the 'external counterpart' of our television set, if communicated in words, would very likely be completely meaningless to us, and would strike us as being the description of something we had never seen.

All this goes to show that actualities are not, in fact, any more fully experienced or perceived than mental events; the perception of them is simply given greater importance for practical and social reasons, and as a consequence of beliefs which we allow to qualify our figurations. Another related point is that 'if objects in my perceptual world are in fact my own creation they can possess not only sensory characteristics but emotional ones, too.' In fact, as one sees oneself as the focal point, the centre, of one's perceptual world, and adjusts all one's actions and ideas in terms of a personal perspective, it is hard to see how any object can be entirely devoid of some kind of emotional quality for the percipient.

We have indeed all lived, in our childhood, in a world where there are no objects. As small children we *knew* that this wall was wicked, that this table disliked us, that this cushion was our friend. We liked certain objects because we felt that they liked us. We felt them to be friendly. The child's cry of 'I don't like it' when faced with a new doll is often truly the cry of 'It doesn't like me', though the child, at that stage, is already wise enough to know that the more accurate statement will be dismissed as fantasy. If we are to face the truth squarely we must also admit that many of our aesthetic judgements could be phrased in terms of the picture, or piece of furniture 'making us feel uncomfortable'. 'I don't know much about art, but I know what I like' could be rephrased in terms of the speaker's actual feelings as 'I don't know much about art but I know what likes me.' Aesthetic judgements are more emotional and participant than we are usually prepared to admit.

If we do admit that for us all, to a greater or lesser degree, all objects have emotional value, we can see that the poem, in assuming the reality of mental events, and in regarding all objects as potentially at least animate, is reflecting the basic structure of our perceptions, rather than qualifying our perceptions with beliefs which force us to think of our perceptions as differing from one another in a fashion in which they, physiologically, do not. We can also see that the primitive and the child are being truer to the facts of experience than others in their belief that the 'name' is inseparable from the object, and that the mental creation of an image is the creation of an actuality, for the mental creation does, in fact, create all the essential elements of the construct derived from an actual counterpart external to the percipient. The major part of the percept is its symbolic value to the percipient, and not its derivation from an inferred external.

The situation is, however, further complicated when we begin to consider time. Sir Russell Brain points out that

> the perceptual world of a single observer possesses not only a space of its own, but also a time of its own, and the time relationship of events in the perceptual world are different from those in the physical world to which they relate.[1]

This is true, not only in the sense that the percipient world, containing mental images as well as constructs with external counterparts, may place events far removed from one another in historical time next to one another, for purposes of examination of given themes, but also in other ways as well. Brain refers to Whitehead and Russell as pointing out that

> owing to the time occupied by the physical processes involved in perception our sense-data must always represent the past state of the object to which they correspond, even when that object is our own body.[2]

This, of course, only becomes really observable when we deal in terms of astronomical time and space, but, whether noticeable ordinarily or not, it exists as a factor in our perception of and relationship with the

---

[1] ibid., p. 39.   [2] ibid., p. 38.

physical world. Yet however long it takes for the physical process of perception to take place, whether it is in terms of light-years or the *n*th part of a second, 'what I am conscious of here and now is a sense-datum which exists contemporaneously in my private perceptual space.'[1] The Theory of Relativity has stated also that time differs according to the position and movement of the observer, so that a further variant must be introduced into our list of factors governing our apprehension of reality. Moreover, even were we able to adjust, by some miracle of mathematical ingenuity, our perceptive process so that we saw the 'now' of whatever object we were looking at, we would still have to face a further complexity, as

> in the perceptual world of a single observer no sense-datum can be the cause of its being perceived, nor of the changes in the nervous system which underlie its perception. The reason is that the coming into existence of the sense-datum and the neural events concerned in this, are contemporary, and contemporary events cannot enter into a mutual causal relationship. . . . The physical world, therefore, is what we infer about the causes of our perceptions, and since it is a product of inference, it is a symbolic representation of the structure of events occurring in space time.[2]

All this adds up to the statement that 'each of us possesses his own private perceptual space, generated by his brain, in which all his perceptual objects, but not their corresponding physical objects, can exist.'[3]

Once we look closely at this situation we can see that the poem emphasizes its existence in several ways. Firstly, it emphasizes the personal nature of each statement of sequence by including emotional and other associations as elements of that sequence. Secondly, it continually juggles with clock-time, so that we are made aware that time is to us more the experience of a sequence or spatial juxtaposition of mental events than the observation of a process of physical causality. Thirdly, it establishes the important part inference plays in our statements about a so-called objective world, by forcing us to draw inferences which are very different from those we would make when being what we call 'objective' about reality. And fourthly, and lastly, as we have seen the whole time-structure of the poem is so different from the time-structure we describe in terms of fidelity to clock-time or to history that, as a whole, the poem suggests that there is a difference between the sense of time we

[1] ibid., p. 39.   [2] ibid., pp. 39–40.   [3] ibid., p. 36.

actually experience and that which we maintain exists in the physical world. Consider the way in which Edwin Muir depicts life's journey in his poem, *Too Much*.

Too Much[1]

No, no, I did not bargain for so much
When I set out upon the famous way
My fathers praised so fondly—such and such
The road, the errand, the prize, the part to play.

For everything is different. Hour and place
Are huddled awry, at random teased and tossed,
Too much piled on too much, no track or trace,
And north and south and road and traveller lost.

Then suddenly again I watch the old
Worn saga write across my years and find,
Scene after scene, the tale my fathers told,
But I in the middle blind, as Homer blind,

Dark on the highway, groping in the light,
Threading my dazzling way within my night.

Here the poet's experience challenges all our usual notions of history and historical progress, and even our assumptions as to the reliability of maps and compasses. Or look at Charles Madge's poem, *Loss*, in which time becomes a fluid ever changing thing.

Loss[2]

Like the dark germs across the filter clean
So in the clear day of a thousand years
This dusty cloud is creeping to our eyes,

Here, as we grow, and are as we have been
Or living give for life some morning tears
The flowering hour bent and unconscious lies.

As in Vienna now, the wounded walls
Silently speak, as deep in Austria
The battered shape of man is without shade

[1] Edwin Muir, *Collected Poems*, Faber and Faber, 1960, p. 163.
[2] Charles Madge, *The Father Found*, Faber and Faber, 1941, p. 38.

So, time in metaphor, tomorrow falls
On Europe, Asia and America,
And houses vanish, even as they were made,

For yesterday is always sad, its nature
Darker than love would wish in every feature.

However true to human ways of perception these poems may be, man, in his non-philosophical moments, has views about time which he cannot help having, whether he believes intellectually in the theories of Private Perceptual Space or not. He is obliged to regard his construct-system in terms of separate objects with limits, for unless he can make clear divisions and definitions he cannot perceive relationship at all. Consequently he conditions his own thought processes by an instinctive belief in the absolute reality of unity. 'One is one and all alone,' as the song has it. This enables him to say that A is not B. If A *is* B, he must create a new unity, AB, and by so doing, think in terms of AB occupying more space than A or B, or, at any rate, having 'more' significance. Quantity is a concept dear to him. The idea of two objects occupying exactly the same space as that occupied by either one of them when existing apart from the other, is foreign to him. One cannot put a pint of beer and a pint of water in one pint jug at the same time. If a conjurer apparently does this, the beholder tends to think immediately of either diminution of the water or expansion of the jug. Again, three things cannot be also one thing, unless the three are to be regarded as *parts* of the one, either facets or particles. (This makes the doctrine of the Trinity, the Three in One, hard for him to perceive.) The idea of size is basic to man. Now it is obvious to anyone at all acquainted with the ideas of today that ideas of size, quantity, and unity, are closely connected with the concept of space-time. The Theory of Relativity points out, among other things, that we can regard all measurements of space as being time measurements. We may argue that we know this black box to be that size and to be singular because of the time we take to survey it, and the coherence of that time-period. We have lifted, measured, looked, over a period of time, and the product of our time spent is to provide the figuration 'One black box'. Our only notion of space comes from the amount of 'time' spent in surveying the pheno-menon, and relating it to other phenomena, which may or may not be arbitrarily created 'standards of measurement'. Yet is clear that, to a child of three, an object may be bigger than it is to a man of twenty. Its actual size has not altered, we say, because our Alpha-thinking shows us that the object has not altered its relationship to the standard of measurement, the ruler. To externalize the standard of space-time measurement is, however, to deny the subjective element in existence, and to deny what is clearly true, that the emotional effect of size is *really* different in the two cases. The child of two may stand easily under the table and find it protecting and guarding, while the man, being 'larger', only finds the table an object of utility which he can master.

Our view that the man is more likely to be viewing the reality than the child is also based upon an assumption—that time is co-extensive with growth, progress towards perfection. Growth 'takes time'. Growth itself is a word dependent upon the concept of size and quantity. Even if we grow in wisdom, we, mentally, tend to regard the quality as having increased in quantity. Decay, also co-extensive with time, is again a quantity-idea. Though we may say that a cheese has 'decayed' even though it has increased in volume, we usually feel that the quality of 'cheese-ness' has lessened in volume; all this shows that man's thought is very much based upon one aspect of his experience of time only— that connected with his sense-figurations regarded as objective. This way of thought even invades the mind when ideas of frequency or intensity occur. Though we may regard intensity as being a concept very different from that of quantity, man usually contrives to think of it in quantity terms. This is more beautiful than that. The heart is full. Frequency, even, is usually imaged mentally in terms of the quantity of occurrence in a given time, which time is imaged in space terms. 'Twenty' a minute means that over a line representing a minute there are placed twenty incidents at regular intervals.

It is impossible to avoid this way of thinking completely; it is too habitual. We can, however, observe that it is *only* thinking, only cerebral, for it is not entirely true to the nature of total perception. Time must, for a standard of measurement to work, be regarded as absolute. Relativity tells us it isn't, just as our own experience tells us it isn't. The honest individual will admit that ten minutes in the dentist's waiting room reading a 1923 copy of the *Stockbreeders Gazette* is a longer period than ten minutes spent reading *Death Strikes Seven* in an armchair by one's own fireside. The concept of quantity suffers a blow here, too, for more mental 'incidents' are likely to have occurred in the second instance than in the first. Quantity, as such, is not correlative with time, as regards the subjective experience of man. Again growth is not co-extensive with time either, for a qualitative increase in understanding can occur momentarily, and can be greater than any increase possible over an extended period of time. Indeed, the shorter the period in which an increase of this kind occurs, the more intense the sensation will be. It is, for example, hard for a man to spend a week gradually growing towards a belief in God; it is much easier for him to grow towards it in five minutes. This is because the important factor in this type of increase is that it must be in terms of the total personality, and few men, except practised yogis and saints, can operate as total personalities over a long period. Indeed, a deep meditation has always the appearance to the meditator of having lasted no time at all . . . or all the time there is. In a famous passage Wordsworth speaks of

> . . . That blessed mood,
> In which the burthen of the mystery,
> In which the heavy and weary weight
> Of all this unintelligible world,
> Is lightened:—that serene and blessed mood,
> In which the affections gently lead us on,—
> Until, the breath of this corporeal frame
> And even the motion of our human blood
> Almost suspended, we are laid asleep
> In body, and become a living soul:
> While with an eye made quiet by the power
> Of harmony, and the deep power of joy,
> We see into the life of things. . . .[1]

These experiences so completely contradict the way in which we normally regard time and space that, if we are to take as our guiding maxim for this investigation truth to human experience, we have to re-orientate our attitudes. We have to admit that, subjectively, two or more objects can occupy the same space. We have to admit that time and space are not absolute. We must agree that measurement can never be true so long as an external standard is regarded as having objective validity. We must indeed attempt to remake our vision of the world.

[1] William Wordsworth, *Tintern Abbey*, ll. 37–49.

FIVE Poetry and Relativity

It is easy to see that poetry, in many ways, attempts to 'remake the world'. The Poetic Symbol, with its total focality, not only presents to us a unity that is pleromatic, but also a unity whose quality of one-ness is effective only in so far as we can accept the contemporaneity and equality of events, myths, and objects usually regarded as being widely separate from each other in time and space. The symbol also forces us to deny the concept of space as a quantity-term, and to perceive it only as an occasion for meaningful relationship. Indeed, poetry establishes the relativity of reality. Relativity is the key word.

This notion of poetry as relativity may be more easily understood if we examine the relationship of poetry to causality, history, and evolution. If we can start with the assumption that the facts of history are, to each person, slightly different, in that each person ends his history with himself (apart entirely from the different interpretations of the established facts) we can move on logically to the statement that each person possesses, as a part of his world view, a different historical consciousness. We can also say that, while the historical events which inform this consciousness can be regarded as having taken place a long time ago, they are nevertheless contemporaneous with the mind which knows them, for they have mental, or subjective, reality. If this is so, the facts of history have a two-fold use. The first is to give a person a sense of 'belonging' in a time-scheme, a tradition, which tradition he has made for himself, as it is his own figuration which he possesses (he can possess nobody else's). The second is to provide him with a series of relationships that he can manipulate in order to work out other relationships. Thus, he can, let us say, by examining the 'history of democracy' work out for himself his own political attitude. Pierre Emmanuel refers to 'the synoptic character of history', and adds that 'It may be read both as a series of events and as a simultaneous drama.'[1]

[1] Pierre Emmanuel, *The Universal Singular*, trans. Erik de Mauny, Grey Walls Press, 1950, p. 162.

Many poets have taken this view of history. Indeed, if we look at the historical poems of Browning, or Tennyson, or Byron, we are immediately aware that the events and attitudes described are mirror-images of events and attitudes of our own day. Frequently a poem placed in a historical setting contrives to suggest not a past event but a recurrent and ever-present phenomenon. This is partly the consequence of using the language of one period to write of the events of another, so that the medium suggests contemporaneity while the content suggests the historical, thus obliging the reader to assent to the poem as an experience that over-rides the limitations of time. An excellent example of the way in which this can be achieved is C.P. Cavafy's poem, *Waiting For The Barbarians*.[1]

Waiting For The Barbarians

What are we waiting for all crowded in the forum ?
    The Barbarians are to arrive today.
Within the Senate-house why is there such inaction ?
The Senators making no laws what are they sitting there for ?
    Because the Barbarians arrive today.
    What laws now should the Senators be making ?
    When the Barbarians come they'll make the laws.

Why did our Emperor get up so early in the morning ?
And at the greatest city gate why is he sitting there now,
Upon his throne, officially, why is he wearing his crown ?
    Because the Barbarians arrive today.
    The Emperor is waiting to receive
    Their Leader. And in fact he has prepared
    To give him an address. On it he has
    Written him down all sorts of names and titles.

Why have our two Consuls gone out, both of them, and the
    Praetors,
Today with their red togas on, with their embroidered togas ?
Why are they wearing bracelets, and all those amethysts too,
And all those rings on their fingers with splendid flashing
    emeralds ?
Why should they be carrying today their precious walkingsticks,
With silver knobs and golden tops so wonderfully carved ?
    Because the Barbarians will arrive today;
    Things of this sort dazzle the Barbarians.

[1] John Mavrogordato (trans.), *The Poems of C. P. Cavafy*, Hogarth Press, 1951, p. 28.

And why are the fine orators not come here as usual
To get their speeches off, to say what they have to say?
    Because the Barbarians will be here today;
    And they are bored with eloquence and speechmaking.
Why should this uneasiness begin all of a sudden,
And confusion. How serious people's faces have become.
Why are all the streets and squares emptying so quickly,
And everybody turning home again so full of thought?
    Because night has fallen and the Barbarians have not come.
    And some people have arrived from the frontier;
    They said there are no Barbarians any more.

And now what will become of us without Barbarians?—
Those people were some sort of a solution.

Cavafy's exploration of history was not simply an exploration of what long ago people thought or did but an exploration of the part they continue to play in his own mental world and in the world of his own construct-system. He saw the 'barbarian' element as necessary to all society and to all individuals. Without the barbarians much motivation is lacking, and no sense of values can remain secure. Moreover he perceived that there is a subjective factor in all perception, and that there will always be a difference between one person's view of past or present events and another's. Knowledge after the event is always, obviously, knowledge of a different event; it is equally true that one person's perception of an event must differ from that of anyone else. Robert Graves, somewhat sardonically, exposed this situation in his poem, *The Persian Version*, which is, like Cavafy's poem, set in past time but presents a recurrent situation:

The Persian Version[1]

Truth-loving Persians do not dwell upon
The trivial skirmish fought near Marathon.
As for the Greek theatrical tradition
Which represents that summer's expedition
Not as a mere reconnaissance in force
By three brigades of foot and one of horse
(Their left flank covered by some obsolete
Light craft detached from the main Persian fleet)

[1] Robert Graves, *Collected Poems 1975*, Cassell, 1975, p. 146.

But as a grandiose, ill-starred attempt
To conquer Greece—they treat it with contempt;
And only incidentally refute
Major Greek claims, by stressing what repute
The Persian monarch and the Persian nation
Won by this salutary demonstration:
Despite a strong defence and adverse weather
All arms combined magnificently together.

Traditionally, of course, the battle of Marathon is regarded as an overwhelming defeat for the Persian army. Graves' poem suggests that historical tradition is based upon a perspective created by a faction rather than by the whole of the people involved. A quick glance through the history books of different countries reveals this. The history of Ireland as told by Irish writers of the late nineteenth century differs considerably from that presented by English writers of the same period. The Russian version of the fall of the Tsars differs from that presented by others. And yet in the majority of these cases the facts are the same. The difference lies in the selection of the facts and in the variation in emphasis. Moreover, as time goes on, we find that current events provide us with changing perspectives on the past. The assassination of President Kennedy altered our perspective upon the assassination of Julius Caesar, and the career of Idi Amin puts that of Papa-Doc Duvalier in a different light.

History is continually changing, for each time we are faced with a new occurrence we revise our perspective of what has gone before. The facts may remain unchallenged, but their significance is continually altering. As with political and social history, so it is with literary tradition, as T. S. Eliot pointed out in his essay, 'Tradition and the Individual Talent'.[1] The crucial passage of his essay runs:

> Yet if the only form of tradition, of handing down, consisted in following the ways of the immediate generation before us in a blind or timid adherence to its successes, 'tradition' should positively be discouraged. We have seen many such simple currents soon lost in the sand; and novelty is better than repetition. Tradition is a matter of much wider significance. It cannot be inherited, and if you want it you must obtain it by great labour. It involves, in the first place, the historical sense, which we may call nearly indispensable to anyone who would continue to be a poet beyond his twenty-fifth year; and

[1] John Hayward (ed.), *T. S. Eliot: Selected Essays*, Penguin Books, 1953, pp. 23–4.

the historical sense involves a perception, not only of the pastness of the past, but of its presence; the historical sense compels a man to write not merely with his own generation in his bones, but with a feeling that the whole of the literature of Europe from Homer and within it the whole of the literature of his own country has a simultaneous existence and composes a simultaneous order. This historical sense, which is a sense of the timeless as well as of the temporal and of the timeless and of the temporal together, is what makes a writer traditional. And it is at the same time what makes a writer most acutely conscious of his place in time, of his own contemporaneity.

No poet, no artist of any art, has his complete meaning alone. His significance, his appreciation is the appreciation of his relation to the dead poets and artists. You cannot value him alone; you must set him, for contrast and comparison, among the dead. I mean this as a principle of aesthetic, not merely historical, criticism. The necessity that he shall conform, that he shall cohere, is not one-sided; what happens when a new work of art is created is something that happens simultaneously to all the works of art which preceded it. The existing monuments form an ideal order among themselves, which is modified by the introduction of the new (the really new) work of art among them. The existing order is complete before the new work arrives; for order to persist after the supervention of novelty, the *whole* existing order must be, if ever so slightly, altered; and so the relations, proportions, values of each work of art toward the whole are readjusted; and this is conformity between the old and the new. Whoever has approved this idea of order, of the form of European, of English literature will not find it preposterous that the past should be altered by the present as much as the present is directed by the past. And the poet who is aware of this will be aware of great difficulties and responsibilities.

This has always been the view of poetry, though nobody formulated that view in a satisfactory fashion before Eliot wrote his essay. Even those poets who deliberately imitated earlier styles equally deliberately attempted to improve upon them and alter them in important respects. This is especially true of those poets who, in the eighteenth century, wrote their *Imitations* and *Translations* of classical poetry. It is equally true of poets who in the seventeenth century vied with each other in the composing of sonnets. The poet, indeed, takes a synoptic view of history and frequently emphasizes history as a system of relationships rather than as a sequence by cutting across the historians' time-order and juxtaposing, let us say, Herod and the Mongol Hordes; St. Jerome may lodge in a cellar of Baudelaire's Paris, and the battle of Waterloo be fought in the same phrase as that of Phillipi. Poetry, in short, emphasizes the contemporaneity of history and sees past events as a system of relationships that includes the present. Robert Lowell, in a collection of poems he called simply *History*, illustrated this point in his poem, *The Republic*[1]

> Didn't Plato ban philosopher-professors,
> the idols of the young, from the Republic?
> And diehard republicans? It wasn't just
> the artist. The Republic! But it never was,
> except in the sky-ether of Plato's thought,
> steam from the horsedung of his city-state—
> Utopia dimmed before the blueprint died. . .
> America planned one . . . Herman Melville
> fixed at that helm, facing a pot of coals,
> the sleet and wind spinning him ninety degrees:
> 'I must not give me up then to the fire,
> lest it invert my fire; it blinded me,
> so did it me.' There's a madness that is woe,
> and there is a wisdom that is madness.

Not all poetry mingles different places and times in the fashion of Lowell, but all poetry is, to some extent, similarly spatial in attitude. It is spatial in its use of cross-temporal juxtapositions and focality. It is also however sequential in that it continually moves in time, from phrase to phrase, verse to verse. It is an act in time (as all acts must be), and it is also a recognition of the relative nature of the time-space sense.

It could even be maintained that the poem attempts to defeat the linear view of language, and to attack the view of life as a simple sequence of events, by means of the image, and attempts to present the experience of sequence by the use of sentences which, necessarily, exist in terms of one thing following another in an ordered manner. The image denies sequence, and the syntax accepts it. A complete denial of the importance of the sense of sequence would, of course, prevent the poem reflecting the true nature of human perception. So-called imagist poems which are made up entirely of the arrangement of images in space rather than in time are often failures if no element of pseudo-narrative or cause-and-effect has crept into the pattern, just as verse that consists simply of rhymed narrative unenriched by any holophrastic element also fails. Both space and sequence must be present in the poem.

The double view of poetry, spatial and sequential, is reflected in many ways in its form and language. The historical consciousness shown in

[1] Robert Lowell, *History*, Faber and Faber, 1973, p. 41.

The Waste Land shows Eliot's attempt to use history as contemporaneous reality, just as his use of straight narrative in the *Journey of the Magi* reveals historical sequence in such a way as to make that sequence an element of today's consciousness of a present situation. Other poets have used other methods to present, in one whole, the sense of movement in time, and the sense of a present condition. The dramatic monologue as used by Browning emphasizes the subjectivity of the view of the speaker, and so presents a state of mind and its historical context. Andrea del Sarto's reminiscences do this job most effectively. The poem must, however, not only present a sequence in such a way as to show its relativist nature, but also reveal the relevance of the events to our own day. For our own day is the only day we have. In other words, in poetry an event must never be merely an event, but always a significant process.

The difference between event and process is important; in it is summarized the difference between history vitally considered and 'historism'. Historism is that attitude towards past events which regards them as separated from today by some finalizing process. 'Queen Anne is dead' is a statement of historism, whereas to any intelligent person it is an obvious untruth. Even the statement that she is dead is a statement that she was, and therefore is, alive in our minds. Historism tends also to provide us with sequences of events in such a way that the sequences have no clear relationship value. We cannot perceive beneath the narrative a relationship that is true of other events; we see only the facts themselves. History tends to deal always in events and phenomena as if these had an existence entirely separate from the perceiving mind. Even the view of history as a pattern of phenomena which is contemporaneous with the observing mind is inclined to take this attitude. Historical reference is reference outward from the perceiver, unless the presentation of the historical material is less important to the message of the whole than is the exploration of the personal sensibility of the supposed speaker.

Poetry is, however, always (if not always ostensibly) concerned to present an individual human experience in terms of that individual's own sensibility, whether that experience is of events of the far past or of the present. It is aware of both sequence and simultaneity in its perception of time, and in this it is obviously very much in sympathy with the theory of evolution, for that theory has the 'double vision' of sequence and simultaneity if we also accept the view of Jung that deep in our unconscious are forces which we contain as inheritance of our most remote past as members of an evolving species. Even if we do not accept the views of

Jung and regard evolution as a series of events which took place over a period of millions of years and culminated in our own births, we cannot separate ourselves entirely from this process, in that each one of us, in our progress from seed to foetus, has undergone a process of evolution, which is similar to, if not identical with, the process viewed in historical terms. We can say that we have actually *been* worm, fish, etc., with more 'scientific' truth than that we have been Julius Caesar and Rameses. We can say that Caesar and Rameses are contained within us as experiences, but cannot really establish our identity with them to the same degree. We are, indeed, biologically involved in other forms of life to a more intimate degree than we are involved in events past. Thus, whereas the idea of history often involves the perceiver in his separation from phenomena, the idea of evolution is liable to involve him more closely in participation. There is a degree of biological 'backing' for the view of the universe as a personalized world, in that we do *in fact* (and not merely in fancy) have the same kind of life as all physical phenomena. Thus we may say that the poetic intuition of a mythopoeic universe can be regarded also as an instinctive perception of a biological actuality.

This attitude of mind is only of importance, however, if it is reflected in the poetry itself. Here again we come across a difference between poetry's view of history and its view of evolution. History is dealing in a process, certainly, but the different parts of that process all appear to be directed, not towards the creation of a fully percipient whole, but towards a social situation that in many ways is far from concerned with perception of reality, and is certainly in a state of fragmentation. Thus, we may feel that the positive, or creative, significance of, say, the Wars of the Roses, cannot be in what they led to, but only in what they *were*. Historical event is important more in terms of the relationships and situations it embodies than in terms of progress. Even the sense of literary tradition is not a sense of continual progress, but a sense of a 'family' of works, each member of which is different, and affected by environment, but no one of which can truly claim to be wiser or more important than the other. The elder members affect the younger, perhaps, but the chain is not a direct one. Wordsworth can be affected more by Milton than by Pope. Donne can affect the twentieth century more than the majority of nineteenth-century poets. The idea of evolution, however, because it results in our believing ourselves to be an end-product, more perfectly made, more wonderful, than any earlier creatures, makes us regard time as a progress, but a progress experienced by each one of us. This can be actually reflected, indeed presented, in linguistic structures.

The organization of the poem is always upon evolutionary lines, even while its references may be destructive of historism and linear time. The poem, in this, accurately presents the dichotomous nature of our experience of time. It does indeed, by presenting the dichotomy in terms of structure, tend to give us control over it, and so make, momentarily, a unified and complete perception possible. It also places the reader in a situation where he can feel himself to be operating with the maximum amount of confidence and vitality, for, in John Dewey's words

> Only when the past ceases to trouble and anticipations of the future are not perturbing is a being wholly united with his environment and therefore fully alive. Art celebrates with peculiar intensity the moments in which the past reënforces the present and in which the future is a quickening of what is now.[1]

The method by which this is achieved requires further explanation. Let us take any poem and look at its structure. First of all is the beginning, the point of origin. This is followed by a development in syntactical or impressionistic terms, which produces the feeling of a process of growth. Even while this continues, however, the words themselves, by using metaphor, and by altering their focality, and by, frequently, deriving their full impact not from immediately preceding words but from other earlier ones, are presenting a 'spatial' attitude towards time. Sometimes this spatial element is so emphatically presented as to leave the evolutionary element dependent entirely upon the fact that words follow one another, and that at the end the poem is completed. One is tempted to think this is the case with Hopkins on occasion. The poem certainly must end with a feeling, not only of a point reached, but of a pattern, a process completed. This process, like the evolutionary process, must have involved many events which do not appear to lead directly towards the logical end of the structure, and must also have given the impression, continually, that the mental events, as they occurred, had real significance *in themselves*, and not merely as parts of a whole, or steps towards a conclusion.

In this way the poem can be said to present the time-sense of man in a more accurate fashion than any other type of linguistic structure. The poem also presents the activity of figuration itself, in that the final moment is the one at which the naming is completed, and the inter-mediate period is spent in experiencing sensations of different kinds,

[1] John Dewey, op. cit., p. 18.

which, as the poem proceeds, are 'combined and constructed', the process only being completed at the very end of the poem. The only difference between the figuration process of reading a poem and that of recognizing an object is that at the end of the activity in one case a name can be produced to sum all up, and in the other this is not the case (unless we regard, as we might, the figuration-process of, say *Kubla Khan*, resulting in the name 'Kubla Khan'). This however is an evasion, as we fully recognize the poem's 'name' as being a blanket word to cover a complex construct of experience, whereas we do not often recognize this as being true of words in general. Thus the perception of poem as figuration results in our being returned yet again to the basics of human perception—each poem is not only an analogue of man, in presenting his time-sense, and his process of perception, but also a direction to return to the 'realities' of experience, rather than to evade them by over-simplification and the casual use of 'names'. Yet the poem itself operates by way of names. There are boxes within boxes. The larger figuration contains hosts of lesser ones, just as the larger evolutionary and spatial presentations contain lesser. In this we may say that the poem has not only man-quality but universe-quality. The universe is composed of such a pattern, the lesser and the larger systems, solar and molecular.

All this might, however, still present a false picture of the situation, were it not that the poem always implies the existence of an individual perceiver, a 'speaker of the poem'. It cannot fail to do this because it is using words, and every time we read words we intuit the presence of a speaker, whether that speaker be a person of strong and complex character, like the speaker of *The Rape of the Lock*, or a rather limited, colourless individual like the speaker of a *Times* leader. This impression of the poem as a person is reinforced, as we have already shown, by the use of holophrastic language, implying the presence of emotion, and by many other factors. Therefore, we realize, in reading the poem, that the space-time situation in which we are involved is closely attached to the perceptions of one personality.

This is important, for we must realize that time is an element of the personality rather than an abstract and external law. It cannot reasonably be described as an illusion (unless we dismiss almost all our constructs as being also illusions) but it can be described as an element of ourselves. Once we realize this, however unconsciously, we are again presented with a relativist view of reality. Our views about history and evolution are only our statement of our own position, a position relative to the dispositions of our own construct-system. This means that, if we are to try and compare, let us say, Neanderthal Man and Renaissance Man in terms of their 'civilization', we can only do it with reference to our own view of civilization, and the results of our comparison can only, in the last resort, be valid in terms of our own construct-system. If we take this a step further we can see that any comparison or judgement we make depends for its 'truth' upon the 'truth' of our own private perceptual space. It is not, therefore, possible for us ever to say that a given action is 'wrong', or that one person is 'wiser' or 'better' than another without adding the rider, 'as far as I am concerned'. Thus the dictum of Oscar Wilde in his Preface to *The Picture of Dorian Gray*—'There is no such thing as a moral or an immoral book. Books are well written, or badly written. That is all'—although disastrously superficial, does indicate the relativist position of the artist with regard to moral and other judgements.

The implications of this are extremely important. They lead one to see that poetry by its very structure must be opposed to dogma of any kind. This is not, of course, to say that an individual poet may not have his own beliefs, or that he has no right to make those beliefs a part of his poetic structures, but that, if he does so, the extent of his obvious commitment to a dogma is liable to vary inversely with the range of his poetic achievement. This appears, at first blush, to be an untenable position, for we instantly think of such works as *Paradise Lost*, Dante's *Inferno*, Wordsworth's *Immortality Ode* and hundreds of successful religious poems. Nevertheless, a careful reading of these poems reveals that while they may be based upon a particular belief, a particular dogma, they are successful not because of their expression of a particular view but because they create for us a sense of *what it is like* to believe. The passion is more important than the proposition. Thus the glory of Dante lies not in his theology but in his vivid and passionate presentation of humanity, and the power of Milton lies not in his presentation of Christian belief but in his portrayal of the drama of essentially human passions. Sometimes, of course, the poet will emphasize the dogma or theory to such an extent that one cannot assent to the poem as an experience without also assenting intellectually to the dogma. If, indeed, the 'spatial' element in the poem, its symbolism and its meta-phorical force depend upon us accepting a ridiculous proposition, then the poem fails. It fails because it is no longer 'poetry'. I. A. Richards has discussed this problem in the following way:

> When the attitude is important, the temptation to base it upon some reference which is treated as established scientific truths are treated is very great, and the poet thus easily comes to invite the destruction of his work;

Wordsworth puts forward his Pantheism, and other people doctrines of Inspiration, Idealism, and Revelation.

The effect is twofold; an appearance of security and stability is given to the attitude, which thus seems to be justified; and at the same time it is no longer so necessary to sustain this attitude by the more difficult means peculiar to the arts, or to pay full attention to form. The reader can be relied upon to do more than his share. That neither effect is desirable is easily seen. The attitude for the sake of which belief is introduced is thereby made not more but less stable. Remove the belief, once it has affected the attitude; the attitude collapses. It may later be restored by more appropriate means, but that is another matter. And all such beliefs are very likely to be removed; their logical connections with other beliefs scientifically entertained are, to say the least, shaky. In the second place these attitudes, produced not by the appropriate means but, as it were by a short cut, through beliefs, are rarely so healthy, so vigorous and full of life as the others. Unlike attitudes normally produced they usually require an increased stimulus every time that they are reinstated. The belief has to grow more and more fervent, more and more convinced, in order to produce the same attitude. The believer has to pass from one paroxysm of conviction to another, enduring each time a greater strain.[1]

This applies to all poems in which the belief is asserted, not as the personal gropings of the speaker resulting from experiences presented by the poem, but as an already existing view which has enabled the perception to take place. Thus, Wordsworth's views in the *Immortality Ode*, being dependent upon a presented experience, do not destroy the poem: we are still 'with' the personality of the speaker, and, whether or not we agree with his beliefs, we can experience their quality, and share in the feeling of the necessity for some form of belief at this point. With Francis Thompson, or with Christina Rossetti, however, we not infrequently find ourselves feeling that the perceptions arose from an already existing dogma, or creed, and if we are unable to share that viewpoint, the poem fails. It is worth noticing, too, that there are many cases, such as the Holy Sonnets of Donne, where the personal involvement of the speaker in his beliefs is so clearly indicated that our possible disagreement with those beliefs cannot affect the intensity of our perception of a man wrestling with them. Consider his Holy Sonnet, *At the round earth's imagined corners blow*. While we must *understand* the story of the Last Judgement in order fully to comprehend the poem, we are under no necessity to *believe* the story, for the poetic force lies in the passionate anguish of the speaker, and in his sense of his own guilt. That anguish

[1] I. A. Richards, *Principles of Literary Criticism*, Routledge and Kegan Paul, 1924, pp. 274–5.

and guilt are universal; they do not depend for their existence upon any particular dogma.

Holy Sonnet[1]

> At the round earths imagin'd corners, blow
> Your trumpets, Angells, and arise, arise
> From death, you numberlesse infinities
> Of soules, and to your scattred bodies goe,
> All whom the flood did, and fire shall o'erthrow,
> All whom warre, dearth, age, agues, tyrannies,
> Despaire, law, chance, hath slaine, and you whose eyes,
> Shall behold God, and never tast deaths woe,
> But let them sleepe, Lord, and mee mourne a space,
> For, if above all these, my sinnes abound,
> 'Tis late to aske abundance of thy grace,
> When wee are there; here on this lowly ground,
> Teach mee how to repent; for that's as good
> As if thou hadst seal'd my pardon, with thy blood.

In this case the validity of the poem lies more in the presentation of a human situation than in the truth or otherwise of the beliefs which have caused this particular situation to exist. In other words, the poem relies upon expressed beliefs only to the extent that these are symptomatic of all beliefs of a certain kind. This leads us to the further qualification that it is the expression of systematized belief that is dangerous. We can share the experience of Francis Thompson's *The Hound of Heaven*, simply because we are not required to believe in Christ, but to share in the attempted escape from a pursuing Truth, a Truth we cannot evade, and this is a common psychological experience. The poem begins:

> I fled Him, down the nights and down the days;
> I fled Him, down the arches of the years;
> I fled Him, down the labyrinthine ways
> Of my own mind; and in the mist of tears
> I hid from Him, and under running laughter.
> Up vistaed hopes I sped;
> And shot, precipitated,
> Adown Titanic glooms of chasmed fears,
> From those strong Feet that followed, followed after.
> But with unhurrying chase,
> And unperturbèd pace,

[1] John T. Shawcross (ed.), *The Complete Poems of John Donne*, Anchor Books, 1967, pp. 340–1.

Deliberate speed, majestic instancy,
    They beat—and a Voice beat
    More instant than the Feet—
'All things betray thee, who betrayest Me.'

    I pleaded, outlaw-wise,
By many a hearted casement, curtained red,
    Trellised with intertwining charities;
(For, though I knew His love Who followèd,
    Yet was I sore adread
Lest, having Him, I must have naught beside)
But, if one little casement parted wide,
    The gust of His approach would clash it to:
Fear wist not to evade, as Love wist to pursue.
Across the margent of the world I fled,
    And troubled the gold gateways of the stars,
    Smiting for shelter on their clangèd bars;
    Fretted to dulcet jars
And silvern chatter the pale ports o' the moon.
I said to Dawn: Be sudden—to Eve: Be soon;
    With thy young skiey blossoms heap me over
    From this tremendous Lover—
Float thy vague veil about me, lest He see!
    I tempted all His servitors, but to find
My own betrayal in their constancy,
In faith to Him their fickleness to me,
    Their traitorous trueness, and their loyal deceit.
To all swift things for swiftness did I sue;
    Clung to the whistling mane of every wind.
    But whether they swept, smoothly fleet,
    The long savannahs of the blue;
    Or whether, Thunder-driven.
They clanged his chariot 'thwart a heaven,
Plashy with flying lightnings round the spurn o' their feet:—
    Fear wist not to evade as Love wist to pursue.
    Still with unhurrying chase,
    And unperturbèd pace,
Deliberate speed, majestic instancy,
    Came on the following Feet,
    And a Voice above their beat—
'Naught shelters thee, who wilt not shelter Me.'[1]

---

[1] *The Poems of Francis Thompson*, Burns, Oates and Washbourne, 1913, p. 89.

What is true of *The Hound of Heaven* is true of many religious poems. We are faced, not with the necessity of sharing a systematized dogmatic creed, an exclusive structure of interpretations of reality, but simply a universal sensation, a feeling of belief itself. And where the poet who himself believes in a dogma refers to that dogma in terms of images which can be read in a more universal fashion, his poem can be successful with people who do not share his tenets, as well as with those that do.

This of course presents a problem of whether the non-Christian reader of, say, *The Hound of Heaven*, reads the true poem or not, as his poem will differ markedly from the poem of the Christian reader. This is something which we will discuss later. At present we must agree that our digression on the effect of incorporating beliefs into poetry supports our contention that poetry itself is distrustful of dogma, as such. The belief about reality must not be separated from the experience of it; and the belief, to be true to perception, must be in personal rather than general terms. As regards morality, therefore, poetry tends to imply that the only judgement that can ever be made of a person's character or actions must be made in terms of that person's own private construct-system. Thus, for the Christian, the result must be that he obeys the injunction to 'Judge Not', and also perceives that the statement that each person has an immortal soul, whether he be Neanderthal or Renaissance man, can be taken to mean that the real stature and the real development of the individual must be seen in terms of that individual, not in terms of external criteria. One might perhaps say that the real progress of the individual is towards the making of a flawless system of relationships within his construct-system, and that it matters very little exactly how many objects are used, or are available to be used, to create this relationship. A circle is a circle, however large or small it be, and whatever the medium in which it is drawn.

Although the above argument may appear to be a digression from our main purpose, the last sentence does return us to one of the characteristics of poetry, and of all art. Faced with a perfect lyric and a perfect epic we are unable to say which is, as art, the most successful. Our only way of doing this is in terms of range of reference, of allusion and philosophical content, and even as we argue in this way we are always uneasily aware that our argument is not entirely true to purely artistic canons. We are often, indeed, reduced to speaking of 'personal taste', or of personal 'agreement' with the viewpoint of one of the works under discussion. Poetry returns us, as soon as we begin to discuss it, to the private nature of all our means of communication, the limited nature of our judgements, the strange autonomy of the individual perception process, the irrationality of our most trusted procedures, and the essential solitariness of the individual. It emphasizes the truth of those scientific hypotheses, based upon (essentially) the comparison of different construct-systems with their external counterparts in such a way that a minimum, but important, agreement between different observers of similar cultural environments can be asserted, and at all points supports the private and subjective experiences of the individual. It does this in terms of its use of language and its spatial and temporal structures, and if we were to characterize the nature of its main impact, we would be obliged to say that it disturbs our working system of approximations with a presentation of reality.

So far our discussion of poetry has led us towards the destruction of shibboleths, rather than the perception of truths. Poetry has been seen as inhabiting a subjective and highly fluid world in which we have not yet found any one stability, save that of the poem itself as a completed pattern. The reason why the poem has this completeness, this 'thing-in-itself-quality', deserves further examination. We can start off by suggesting that the poem must, to succeed, make its own system of events significant of existing and fundamental relationships, and not merely present a significant method. The form itself, the total structure, must have relationships inherent in it which correspond to something basic in man's mode of perception. So far we have seen that many aspects of poetic language do correspond to the true nature of human perception, and by so doing set themselves up in opposition to generally accepted notions about time, language, and reality. Can we now examine the nature of poetic form in more detail, taking as our rough definition of form 'those aspects of poetry which most immediately and obviously present ideas of pattern and arrangement' ? There are many factors which go to make the poem a complete whole, and give it that formal singularity without which it cannot communicate on any save superficial levels. The most obvious one is, perhaps, the most important. The poem is given coherence by possessing a unified 'personality'. No matter what poem one takes up, it must impress with a 'tone of voice'. This tone is given its qualities by distinctive turns of speech, rhythmical effects, the nature of the imagery, and, indeed, all other aspects of the writing, and yet it can be recognized as a quality in itself.

This alone is inadequate, of course. Otherwise any twenty lines of *Paradise Lost* could be regarded as an entire poem. It is reinforced by the rhythmic patterns, taking rhythm to mean more than mere variations of aural pitch and emphasis. Once a rhythm, an 'ordered variation of change', has been established, it becomes possible to notice the gradual construction of a pattern in rhythmic terms. The ground rhythm may be a metrical one. This gives shape to lines and paragraphs. A further rhythm may be in terms of recurrent images or image-categories, or in terms of narrative; it may be in terms of any linguistic element capable of repetition and recurrence.

This rhythmic quality has two effects. The first is pseudo-mathematical. Given the first few numbers in a series it is possible to determine the remainder, provided the relationship between the first ones is not merely haphazard. Thus, presented with a certain rhythmic series, the reader intuits the ensuing pattern. Consequently he feels that a 'system' is being presented, and anticipates a whole rather than a fragment. Poets have used this fact over and over again in order to provoke surprise by varying the set pattern once it has been established, thus giving the poem that wayward quality typical of organic life. Thomas Hardy takes this device farther than most poets, as in *On the Way*:

On The Way[1]

The trees fret fitfully and twist,
Shutters rattle and carpets heave,
Slime is the dust of yestereve,
    And in the streaming mist
Fishes might seem to fin a passage if they list.

    But to his feet,
    Drawing nigh and nigher
    A hidden seat,
    The fog is sweet
    And the wind a lyre.

A vacant sameness grays the sky,
A moisture gathers on each knop
Of the bramble, rounding to a drop,
    That greets the goer-by
With the cold listless lustre of a dead man's eye.

    But to her sight,
    Drawing nigh and nigher
    Its deep delight,
    The fog is bright
    And the wind a lyre.

[1] Thomas Hardy, *Collected Poems*, Macmillan, 1930, pp 591–2.

The rhythmic patterns themselves also produce this organic quality. Man is highly conscious of rhythm, not only in his pattern-wise judgements and in his Alpha-thinking, but in his breath and pulse. Thus the rhythmic elements not only indicate possible completion of a pattern, but also convey the essentially human nature of the statement presented.

The linguistic structure also suggests the possibility of completeness by its very method of speech; when all aspects of the personality are brought into play—the most and the least conscious alike—the reader recognizes that his own personality is required to perceive with all its functions, and consequently, again, a perfect whole is expected to result. In fact, the completeness of the method makes inevitable anticipation of the completion of the pattern.

Once this has been established the poem can be concluded in many ways, according to which rhythm is the dominant one. The image pattern can end a 'movement' at the same point as the metric pattern and the syntactical pattern. This in itself is sufficient to make a paragraph or break in the poem, wherever it occurs. If it occurs at a point where all other subsidiary patterns have also reached the end of a movement, the poem completes itself. We can say, in fact, that the formal singularity, the 'thing-in-itself' quality, depends to a considerable extent upon the relationship between the various rhythms involved. The poem fulfils its own expectancies while not infrequently frustrating the expectancies of the language system. John Berryman's *Dream Song 112* is a good example of a highly rhythmical poem whose rhythms and diction seem almost wayward, and yet which clearly fulfils its destiny at the end of its statement and completes a pattern.

Dream Song 112[1]

> My framework is broken, I am coming to an end,
> God send it soon. When I had most to say
> my tongue clung to the roof
> I mean of my mouth. It is my Lady's birthday
> which must be honoured, and has been. God send
> it soon.
>
> I now must speak to my disciples, west
> and east. I say to you, Do not delay
> I say, expectation is vain.
> I say again, It is my Lady's birthday
> which must be honoured. Bring her to the test
> at once.

[1] John Berryman, *The Dream Songs*, Farrar, Straus and Giroux, 1969, p. 129.

> I say again, It is my Lady's birthday
> which must be honoured, for her high black hair
> but not for that alone:
> for every word she utters everywhere
> shows her good soul, as true as a healed bone,—
> being part of what I meant to say.

The completion of a rhythmic pattern is not, of course, the only necessary attribute of the poem for it to achieve formal singularity. Every poem implies, in one way or another, that it has chosen for itself a particular area of thought or feeling to explore. In implying this it, of necessity, implies that the area has certain limits, which limits are gradually brought into clearer definition as the poem proceeds. Once all these limits have been indicated the poem can be completed. The poem proceeds by means of a constant series of applied limitations—limitations of tone, subject, syntax, rhythm, argument, and so forth. There are many poems which make use of this aspect of poetic structure in order to reach a dramatic conclusion. The limits are all defined, but the answer to the problem posed has not been discovered. A rhythmic whole has been made. Consequently the poem ends, if not upon an actual, explicitly phrased, question, then certainly upon a questioning note. Theodore Spencer's poem, *The Inflatable Globe*, is very interesting in this respect. The story told has a shape which appears inevitable, and the rhythm and the rhyme scheme create a clear and obsessive pattern.

The Inflatable Globe[1]

> When the allegorical man came calling,
> He told us all he would show us a trick,
> And he showed us a flat but inflatable ball.
> 'Look at this ball,' he told us all;
> 'Look at the lines marked on this ball.'
> We looked at the ball and the lines on the ball:
> England was red, and France was blue;
> Germany orange and Russia brown:
> 'Look at this ball,' he told us all,
> 'With a blow of my breath I inflate this ball.'
> He blew, and it bounced, and bouncing, falling,
> He bounced it against the wall with a kick.
> 'But without my breath it will flatten and fall,'

[1] Oscar Williams, op. cit., p. 226.

Said the allegorical man; and down
Flat came his hand and squashed the ball,
And it fell on the floor with no life at all
Once his breath had gone out of the ball . . .
It seemed to us all a stupid trick.

In this poem we also have another kind of pattern, which consists of the
tension between allegory and symbol. In allegory the image is to be read
as signifying one particular quality; the lady stands for chastity and
nothing else, and the knight in armour for Christian fortitude and
nothing else. Allegory is therefore very linear in its operation. The
symbol is, as we know, intended to arouse many possibilities of meaning.
In this poem that which is presented as allegorical is in fact symbolic and
that which appears to be symbolic is in fact allegorical. I made this point
in an earlier book when I wrote:

> Although the man is described as allegorical, it is the ball whose significance
> can be defined. The ball is the world, and that is obvious. The man, however,
> defies accurate definition. A Christian might say he was God. Someone else
> might say Love—or, indeed, any quality which seems to him to be the most
> important constituent of life, and that which gives life significance. It could
> be that he is simply Man; without Man the world is meaningless. The poem
> itself does not make any one interpretation inevitable, and consequently the
> allegorical man is a symbol, although the ball is allegorical.[1]

This poem is, in some ways, an oddity, but it does illustrate very clearly
the way in which a poem can be a rhythmic whole, and a narrative unity,
and possess a tight pattern of tension which contains both linear and
spatial elements. All successful poems have these attributes, even if they
are not narratives, for they all present a sequence. This cannot of course
be proved without making a much longer and more thorough survey of
poems than we have space for. We might however say again that the
successful poem achieves its unique formal vitality by means of the
relationship between its various rhythmic and limiting devices, and return
to a point made earlier. This is the point that a thing-in-itself quality is,
essentially, a world-in-itself quality. A world-in-itself quality implies a
personal quality. A poem must be a person. The only way in which an
event, incident, or unit of any kind can be also a universal is for it to
possess human characteristics, for the universe is to each one of us a
subjective figuration, and its centre is the human psyche.

[1] Robin Skelton, *Poetry*, Teach Yourself Series, English Universities Press,
1963, p. 71.

SIX Poetry and Explanation

Earlier in this book I maintained that because man understands and perceives entirely by making patterns, the poem, by being so obviously a pattern, presents him with an experience embodying a formal indication of the way in which all experience is perceived. The poem not only presents a pattern of experience but also an experience of pattern itself. It is also, I think, true that the poem, because it communicates in intuitive, emotional, sensual, and intellectual ways, and because it involves its reader in sharing as well as recognizing an experience, presents a kind of 'total' perception which is not available elsewhere. The reader undergoes and observes an experience at the same time. Moreover, the poem, because it is invariably of a pseudo-dramatic nature—requiring the reader to intuit the presence of an often closely defined 'speaker'—forces us to indulge in a degree of impersonation; we are made to 'become' the poem. The poem is a pattern which presents us with the speech of a personality caught in the very act of perception, and we, as readers, both become and understand that personality and that act, thus achieving a sense of 'wholeness' in our response to, and apprehension of, experience, which approximates to the neoplatonic 'Fourth Way of Knowing'.

In arguing this I was doing little more than rehearse attitudes presented by many past poets and critics. I was also coming very near to accepting Susanne Langer's view that the mode of poetry is more important than its messages, that poetry is a 'morphology of feeling', that the poem's job is to present the *way* we perceive rather than *what* we perceive, that 'the medium is the message'. Susanne Langer maintains that

> the 'facts' have no existence apart from values; their emotional import is part of their appearance; they cannot, therefore, be stated and then 'reacted to'. They occur only as they seem—they are *poetic facts*, not neutral facts towards which we are invited to take a poetic attitude.[1]

[1] Susanne K. Langer, *Feeling and Form*, Routledge and Kegan Paul, 1953, p. 223.

This is one case against certain modes of criticism, and if we add that these 'poetic facts' derive their import as much from their positioning in a rhythmic whole as from their individual power, we can see that much criticism in neglecting these factors is simply criticism of a poem-substitute. All too few critics realize with A. S. P. Woodhouse, in his essay, 'The Historical Criticism of Milton', that

> the poem is not a record of experience: it *is* the experience. It is not a record of thought: it is compacted of those
>> *thoughts that voluntary move*
>> *Harmonious numbers,*
> and that reach full realization only in them.[1]

Those critics who concentrate upon exegesis, who spend pages analysing the message, the content of the poem, as if the poet were engaged in deliberately obscuring a thought, are not studying *poetry* at all. They are studying, perhaps, the history of ideas, or sociology, or even social anthropology, but not poetry. Unfortunately today they are in the majority.

Our object, however, is to try to see what the true poem actually is, and in doing this we must try to avoid emphasizing any one element at the expense of considering others. Susanne Langer describes poetry as creating 'a virtual "life"', or, as is sometimes said "a world of its own".[2] That phrase is not altogether happy because it suggests the familiar notion of 'escape from reality', but a world created as an artistic image is given us to look at, not to live in, and in this respect is radically unlike the neurotic's 'private world'.

Here Dr Langer is perhaps making a mistake. The world of the poem is important simply because it *is* the world we live in. We can in fact 'live' in poetry with a more aware intensity than we do normally, but the experience of the poem's 'life' only differs from 'real life' in that we realize that our experience is a mental construct, whereas we suppose, in 'real life' that it is a mirror-image of externals which we perceive directly through the senses as well as through our beliefs, emotions, and intellectual actions. Nevertheless Susanne Langer's views lead her towards a conclusion with which we must be in sympathy. She points out that:

To treat *anything* that deserves the name of poetry as factual statement which is simply 'versified', seems to me to frustrate artistic appreciation from the

[1] In William J. Hardy and Max Westbrook, *Twentieth Century Criticism: The Major Statements*, The Free Press, 1974, p. 336.
[2] Susanne K. Langer, op. cit., p. 228.

outset. A poem always creates the symbol of a feeling, not by recalling objects which would elicit the feeling itself, but by weaving a pattern of words—words charged with meaning, and coloured by literary associations—akin to the dynamic pattern of the feeling (the word 'feeling' here covers more than a 'state'; for feeling is a process, and may have not only successive phases, but several simultaneous developments; it is complex and its articulations are elusive).[1]

This leads to the statement that poetry is a 'non-discursive symbolic form', and to the view that 'the laws which govern the making of poetry are not those of discursive logic. They are "laws of thought" as truly as the principles of reasoning are; but *they never apply to scientific pseudo-scientific (practical) reasoning.'*

It is here that one begins to smell a rat, and one's doubts become stronger when one reads that:

> in poetry there is no genuine logical argument; this again is paralleled by the speciousness of reasoning in dreams. The 'fixation of belief' is not the poet's purpose; his purpose is the creation of a virtual experience of belief or of its attainment. His 'argumentation' is the semblance of thought process, and the strain, hestitation, frustation, or the swift subtlety of mental windings, or a sense of sudden revelation, are more important elements in it than the conclusion.[2]

The logical conclusion to this statement, no matter how subtly we qualify all our approaches to the problem of 'pure poetry', is, as Donald Davie has explained:

> . . . if the structures of expression are to be more interesting to the reader than the structures of experience behind them, the only way to induce the right sort of attention in the reader is to have nothing behind them at all, that is, to have poems that are meaningless. The only alternative is to have poems that talk about themselves. . . .[3]

It is obvious that we cannot honestly agree that poetry never gives us information in the same way as prose. It may do other things as well, but, surely, we learn something of the topography of the Lake District from Wordsworth, and a good deal of philosophy from Donne, Shelley, and Eliot. Rupert Brooke's *Grantchester* may be the presentation of a state of mind, but the places he describes exist, and who can deny the presence of

[1] ibid., p. 230.   [2] ibid., p. 243.
[3] Donald Davie, *Articulate Energy*, Routledge and Kegan Paul, 1955, p. 93.

logical argument in Browning or Pope ? Dare we say of all poems that they are non-discursive ? Are there not some good poems which do clearly include 'scientific of pseudo-scientific (practical) reasoning' ?

It may be that the informative, didactic, argumentative, discursive aspect of poetry is subordinate to other aspects but it is clear that there have been many poets who felt that their poems should be as much vehicles as organisms. There is the 'public poem'—the poem written in order to say something to an audience. Are we to deny the name of poetry to *Absolom and Achitophel*, *De Rerum Natura* and *The Vision of Judgement ?* The question is absurd.

We have reached a point, however, when we can isolate two main tendencies in poetry—that towards didacticism, the apparent main object of the poem being the presentation of facts and opinions which are important in themselves, and that towards reflexiveness, the main object of the poem being the presentation of the writer's or speaker's state of mind.

The didactic element in poetry requires little examination from us at this time. It is clear enough when the poem's argument, or factual content, is the main part of its presentation. Nevertheless, we can clarify the concept of didacticism a little by dividing it into two kinds. The first and most obvious kind is where the poem gives us the impression that its justification lies in the way in which its exploration of experience has resulted in a statement of belief, a moral, religious, or sociological conclusion. The second kind is where the poem suggests that its justification lies mostly in its presentation of 'information', which has an importance entirely distinct from the importance it has for the speaker himself, involved as he is in exploring the nature of his own relationship to phenomena. Thus Gray's *Elegy* is didactic in the first sense, and Johnson's *Vanity of Human Wishes* is didactic in both senses of the term. It could, however, be argued that in both these poems there is a reflexive element also, in that both are obviously concerned to present an impor-tant 'state of mind', and both comment obliquely upon their own procedures and the way in which the viewpoint shifts as the structure moves towards completion. It is perhaps a question of emphasis, and the more difficult to examine because all poems contain some element of impersonal 'information', for they have to present a certain number of pseudo-objective 'facts' for us to be able to enter into a world of the poem at all. Perhaps we can get nearer to the heart of the problem by looking at the reflexive element, rather than the didactic.

A poem concerned with the nature of perception, as are all poems by their very structure, may comment upon as well as present the perceptual process. In so doing it is likely to find itself commenting specifically upon the 'poetic' perception, simply because it is only by way of poetry that we can see, in verbal form, the true nature of our relationship to reality. Thus we get such superb poems as Wallace Stevens' *Notes Towards a Supreme Fiction* and Archibald MacLeish's *Ars Poetica* which, while being a didactic poem in one sense, for it is a poem intended to tell the reader about the nature of poetry, is also reflexive in that the poem is itself an instance of the way in which poetry, as described by the poem, operates. Moreover *Ars Poetica*, while giving us a lesson in poetics, does so in the language of poetry, by spatial and not by linear language.

Ars Poetica[1]

A poem should be palpable and mute
As a globed fruit,

Dumb
As old medallions to the thumb,

Silent as the sleeve-worn stone
Of casement ledges where the moss has grown—

A poem should be wordless
As the flight of birds.

*

A poem should be motionless in time
As the moon climbs,

Leaving, as the moon releases
Twig by twig the night-entangled trees,

Leaving, as the moon behind the winter leaves,
Memory by memory the mind—

A poem should be motionless in time
As the moon climbs

*

A poem should be equal to:
Not true.

[1] Archibald MacLeish, *Collected Poems*, Houghton Mifflin, 1963, pp. 50-1.

For all the history of grief
An empty doorway and a maple leaf.

For love
The leaning grasses and two lights above the sea—

A poem should not mean
But be.

This poem is exceptional in devoting itself entirely to the presentation of the nature of poetry. It is more usual for the comment upon the nature of the poetic attitude to be part of a larger referential whole, though it may be the central part. Wordsworth's *The Prelude* is a case in point, as is Whitman's *Leaves of Grass*. Such works are using didactic techniques in order to serve a reflexive purpose. These are both poems that 'talk about themselves' while also presenting descriptions of and comments upon events in the external world.

Some poems 'talk about themselves' by commenting upon their own structures. This is apparent when we consider Pope's *Essay on Criticism* or Byron's *Don Juan*, which opens with delightful candour:

Canto the First

I

I want a hero: an uncommon want,
   When every year and month sends forth a new one,
Till, after cloying the gazettes with cant,
   The age discovers he is not the true one:
Of such as these I should not care to vaunt,
   I'll therefore take our ancient friend Don Juan—
We all have seen him, in the pantomime,
Sent to the devil somewhat ere his time.

II

Vernon, the butcher Cumberland, Wolfe, Hawke,
   Prince Ferdinand, Granby, Burgoyne, Keppel, Howe,
Evil and good, have had their tithe of talk,
   And fill'd their sign-posts then, like Wellesley now;
Each in their turn like Banquo's monarchs stalk,
   Followers of fame, 'nine farrow' of that sow:
France, too, had Buonaparté and Dumourier
Recorded in the Moniteur and Courier.

III

Barnave, Brissot, Condorcet, Mirabeau,
   Pétion, Clootz, Danton, Marat, La Fayette,
Were French, and famous people, as we know;
   And there were others, scarce forgotten yet,
Joubert, Hoche, Marceau, Lannes, Dessaix, Moreau,
   With many of the military set,
Exceedingly remarkable at times,
But not at all adapted to my rhymes.

Some poems contrive to 'talk about themselves' by making it impossible for the reader to suppose that any of the references in the poem are to things other than matters of symbolic importance to the speaker, whom we get to know as the poem proceeds, or as we read the whole of the poet's canon. The references 'outward' in Yeats' *Sailing to Byzantium* appear to be to matters which are important as illuminations of the mind and feeling of the poem, rather than important in themselves:

Sailing To Byzantium[1]

I

That is no country for old men. The young
In one another's arms, birds in the trees
—Those dying generations—at their song,
The salmon-falls, the mackerel-crowded seas,
Fish, flesh, or fowl, commend all summer long
Whatever is begotten, born, and dies.
Caught in that sensual music all neglect
Monuments of unageing intellect.

II

An aged man is but a paltry thing,
A tattered coat upon a stick, unless
Soul claps its hands and sing, and louder sing
For every tatter in its mortal dress,
Nor is there singing school but studying
Monuments of its own magnificence;
And therefore I have sailed the seas and come
To the holy city of Byzantium.

[1] W. B. Yeats, *Collected Poems*, Macmillan, 1950, p. 217.

III

O sages standing in God's holy fire
As in the gold mosaic of a wall,
Come from the holy fire, perne in a gyre,
And be the singing-masters of my soul.
Consume my heart away; sick with desire
And fastened to a dying animal
It knows not what it is; and gather me
Into the artifice of eternity.

IV

Once out of nature I shall never take
My bodily form from any natural thing,
But such a form as Grecian goldsmiths make
Of hammered gold and gold enamelling
To keep a drowsy Emperor awake;
Or set upon a golden bough to sing
To lords and ladies of Byzantium
Of what is past, or passing, or to come.

This is a poem about the compulsion to make poetry. In the twentieth century there are many such poems. This is altogether reasonable, for if poetry is important then it is important to write about it, and if the poetic method of using language is the only one which corresponds to the way in which we actually perceive, then our explorations of poetry must, in order to be thorough, *be* poetry. Nevertheless, there is a weakness here, and a weakness that is largely the result of the society in which the poet finds himself. It is worth noticing that in these primitive societies in which the poet is an accepted member of the community there are very few poems about poetry itself. There is little necessity for them. It is also worth noticing that in these communities the ordinary approach to external reality is much more akin to the poetic than in more 'civilized' communities. The poet, indeed, is simply providing a linguistic presentation in a formal pattern of a commonly accepted and universally understood approach to reality. He is the voice of his community, and important as a magician, in that by providing the pattern he also provides a sense of control, of mastery, over the elements of that pattern.

Even as we notice this situation, however, we must also recognize that the poetry of the primitive is, to us, often rather thin. It often seems to consist of a series of accepted poetic epithets strung together, a pattern of symbols and images merely. We, of course, cannot experience these symbols as the primitive does: we cannot, without help, accept the power of the symbolic word. Moreover, despising as we do the instinctive participation of the primitive and the child, we demand that our poems should include some form of sophisticated thinking, some generalizing idea, some philosophical content, and, being unable to accept the significance of mere experience without intellectual argument, we insist that the poem should have something to 'say'. Three-quarters of the critical examination of poetry is devoted to 'proving' that the successful poem has something to 'say', has a contribution to make to thought. Where it is difficult to prove this, the critic either downgrades the poet concerned (Herrick, for example), or falls back upon a historical approach, or one which allows him to pretend that a poem is simply a form of pseudo-music, which is ridiculous.

It is this situation which is responsible for the creation of many poems about poetry. They are defensive manoeuvres. The poet must justify his own existence, and must also appear to be talking 'about' something. He must indeed pretend, to some extent, to be able to separate himself from the experience he is presenting, otherwise the community will regard his work as being meaningless, without object, and unimportant, and he, being himself a product of that community and, in part, in instinctive agreement with it, will himself find his own poems not worth the effort of composition. This leads the poet towards both social comment and didacticism, and towards explicit reflexiveness. The two tendencies I have outlined are indeed the product of modern civilization.

This is not to say that there are not other reasons for a poet's moving in either of the two indicated directions, of course. It is, however, to suggest that we cannot view poetry in isolation from the community in which it is written, nor prevent ourselves judging it in terms of its relationship to the community in which we believe ourselves to be living now. A poem is only a good poem if it presents the manner of our real perception, and it cannot present this manner if it omits to consider the way in which we modify our experience by our beliefs, or regard our private construct-systems as being essentially mirror images of external reality. If poetry is to present the real texture of experience, it must present, not only the dichotomy of sensations of space and sequence, but also that of perception as both private experience and public reference. That is to say, it must show that we make use of private construct-systems in order to manipulate inferred external counterparts, and must indicate that, whether or not we are concerned to explore our own individual construct-systems, we cannot help believing that they have some reference to a reality other than ourselves. Moreover, the result of any successful exploration of a situation is the understanding and controlling of it as an aid to further exploration, and an incitement to action; we can only describe our actions adequately by relating them to something we regard as outside ourselves.

Thus poems that talk about themselves, while revealing the uneasiness of the poet's position in modern society, also avoid presenting, in any real fashion, that part of the nature of perception which is directed towards a belief about the nature of inferred externals, and those poems that are pure because 'meaningless' omit an important aspect of the human relationship to perception. Nevertheless, this reference to externals cannot be regarded as being the central motive of the poem. Dewey says:

> In an intellectual experience, the conclusion has value on its own account. It can be extracted as a formula or as a 'truth', and can be used in its independent entirety as factor and guide in other enquiries. In a work of art there is no such single self-sufficient deposit. The end, the terminus, is significant not by itself but as the integration of the parts. It has no other existence.[1]

We have come a long way round to this statement, but the journey has been instructive. It appears that one of the factors in the poem's quality as a 'thing-in-itself' is the integrating effect of the 'meaning'. The subject of the poem being, in a way, perception itself, it is difficult to see how it could achieve any conclusion without some control-pattern. The rhythmic elements may, as we have already pointed out, tend to make a certain kind of completion possible, but these are rarely strong enough to do the job by themselves. Moreover metrical patterns tend to be repetitive, as do image patterns and syntactical arrangement: they recur throughout the poem, often overlapping and counterpointing one another. It is possible, however, by isolating a series of concepts, to present a pattern which has clear limits. It may be, therefore, that the poem's 'message' is its main control factor.

Although we may regard the 'message' or 'meaning' as a control factor, rather than as a basic motive, we must not fall into the trap of believing that the phrase 'main control factor' means that the presence of this factor need be immediately obvious to the reader. There must be some impression of 'message', and the reader must perceive the presence of some 'meaningful' arrangement of words, but the semblance of

[1] John Dewey, op. cit., p. 55.

meaning is as important as real meaning, so far as the control function is concerned, and this can be provided very largely by syntax. Syntax, being sequential, arouses notions of progress. Logic is itself a progress. If the poem, by the arrangement of sentences in such a fashion as to mimic the usual formation of argumentative logical language, can suggest the presence of intellectual movement, it may be able to do without all but a small fragment of 'meaning'. This is the case with many rhapsodical lyrics, with much of the work of Swinburne, and with almost the whole of Ginsberg's *Howl*. In this case, of course, I am talking about 'meaning' as conceptual thought; the poem may make many comments upon the external world, as does Ginsberg in *Howl*, but the conceptual thought of the whole poem can be summed up in a short sentence. One cannot read *Howl* for its philosophical content!

One might well wonder why poets should deliberately create works which have little philosophical content, little logical meaning. One reason is, I believe, poetry's attempt to emphasize the nature of language as more than a vehicle for factual information and philosophical argument, and to make it difficult for the reader to create a substitute-poem by pretending that the poem is merely the vehicle for a conceptual 'message'. The creation of substitute-poems is not simply an academic activity. The ordinary reader, accustomed to think of language as a means of communicating precise connotations, is inclined to evade the experience of ambiguity and holophrasis wherever possible. He distrusts the statement that derives its impact purely from its emotional and associative quality: he may 'enjoy' it but he does not like to regard it as 'true'. A 'true' statement is one that can be evaluated entirely in terms of fidelity to inferred externals. Moreover, in any individual the act of recognition has become so automatic that it is no longer an act of true perception, but an automatic reflex, no matter how many beliefs and associations are in fact involved, at an unconscious level, in the recognizing process. Once the individual recognizes that a picture contains the form of a man and a horse, he regards that picture as if it were a substitute for a 'real' man and horse, and judges it according to the accuracy of its delineation, its reproductive activity. In this way he avoids the necessity of exploring textural and tonal relationships, and does not, indeed, see the painting as a painting at all. The same thing occurs with regard to poetry. Very few people can read the *Immortality Ode* without supposing that the poem is merely an expression of a philosophical attitude. Once they have understood the 'message' they read the poem as if it were only a rather musical way of stating that 'message', and instead of experiencing all the rhythmic relationships, all the varying appeals to different forms of perception, regard the 'poetic bits' as to some extent irrelevant to the poem's purpose. 'Recognition [says Dewey] is too easy to arouse vivid consciousness. There is not enough resistance between new and old to secure consciousness of the experience that is had.'[1] We have already shown how, by the use of metaphor, poetry forces its readers to experience the holophrastic nature of language and therefore to perceive the presence of emotion. We must be clear, however, that, because the reader is obliged to experience the holophrastic nature of language in order to understand the metaphor, he actually *feels* emotional disturbance. Metaphor thus provides that 'resistance' which Dewey thinks necessary, and forces the reader to assent to the poem's validity.

The question of the nature of the reader's 'assent' to statements in or outside poetry is important. First of all let us consider the kind of assent given to the statement, 'The sky is blue.' The reader can check this by memory or even, possibly, by looking out of the window. If the statement is more particular and detailed as, for example, in the phrase, 'The blood-smeared beak of the gull', he may hesitate a moment before he recalls having seen gulls with red-tipped beaks and then it is not difficult for him to assent to the validity of the phrase. If however the statement is 'Her hands pull stars down from the sky' there is no way in which he can check this against remembered observations. If he is to continue reading the poem and understanding it he must assent blindly. He must trust the poem. He will find it easier to trust the poem if the statement with which he is faced contains elements that are familiar to him from his previous reading, or from the world of his dreams and fantasies. It will be easier for him to accept the statement, 'Her hands were the roots of trees' than 'Her hands broke like glass' because countless cartoons and fairy stories have utilized the similarity of shape between fingers and roots and branches, and there are many stories of tree-maidens and of maidens becoming trees, whereas glass hands are much less familiar to him. Nevertheless simply because 'Her hands broke like glass' requires him to accept the statement without reference to anything outside the poem's own vision, that statement is likely to have, in itself, more emotional power than the other one. It demands, in its unfamiliarity, such a total revision of the normal associations that it causes an intense emotional disturbance. Frequently, a reader will find himself unable to assent to statements which present the necessity of emotional upheaval;

[1] ibid., p. 53.

he will mutter 'nonsense' as many did at the early poems of Dylan Thomas and at the work of the surrealist poets. He will, being unable to recognize anything at all, refuse to abandon his need to recognize and accept the necessity of perceiving. He will as it were refuse to *create* experience, refuse to participate in the poem, and yet in order to perceive, Dewey tells us,

> . . . a beholder must *create* his own experience. And his creation must include relations comparable to those which the original producer underwent. They are not the same in any literal sense. But with the perceiver, as with the artist, there must be an ordering of the elements of the whole that is, in form, although not in details, the same as the process of organization the creator of the work consciously experienced.[1]

Clearly, the problem of the poet, if he is to produce work which forces his readers to experience real perception, is how to make recognition difficult and perception inevitable. He must not only provide images which make emotional rather than intellectual assent necessary but must also obstruct the path of any reader who is looking for a series of definite conceptual meanings arranged in a logical sequential form. The poem should give an immediate impression of having a 'message' function, in order to achieve unity, but not more than an impression need be provided at the most accessible 'levels' of the poem.

One way of obstructing the seeker after linear or purely conceptual statements is to present the 'message' of the poem in symbols which are (by definition) rich in associative power and yet not so attached to existing dogmas as to be capable of immediate and superficial allegorical interpretation. This is a method used by W. B. Yeats, as we can easily see from re-reading *Sailing to Byzantium* which we looked at earlier. Yeats was, however, actually utilizing a traditional system of symbols and allusions, and recent criticism of his work, unflagging in its exploration of neoplatonic philosophy, has gone far towards proving that as soon as the philosophic system behind the symbol structures is widely known, the reader substitutes allegory for symbolic narrative, and easy intellectual approximations replace complex dynamic spheres of meaning. Thus, as long as religion was a central part of the life of this country, and associated with strong ideas of tragedy, sin, suffering, salvation, cruelty, passion, expiation, and so forth, poets could use words like Christ or Cross, and provide the reader with a sense of complex perception. When

[1] ibid., p. 54.

religion became less involved in the consciousness and in the private irrational fears and hopes of the individual beset by constant threats of disease, plague, starvation, and war, without at all understanding the origin of these disorders, then these words began to lose their force. Today only a minority of readers can read the devotional poetry of earlier centuries without replacing the symbolism by superficial allegory.

Another obstructive technique is that of fragmentation. The poem can be constructed in such a way that it is impossible to regard it as a logical conceptual progress, even though the language used suggests that a strong element of message is present. This is true of *The Waste Land*, and of much of Rimbaud, Corbière, Laforgue, and Pound. The piling up of apparently random images unconnected by any process of causality, while presenting poetry as an arrangement in space rather than as a narrative sequence, also forces the reader to explore in depth rather than 'read off' the 'message' in a quick and superficial manner.

Joseph Frank in his essay, 'Spatial Form in Modern Literature' refers to 'aesthetic form' in modern poetry as being

> based on a space-logic that demands a complete reorientation in the reader's attitude toward language. Since the primary reference of any word-group is to something inside the poem itself, language in modern poetry is really reflexive. The meaning-relationship is completed only by the simultaneous perception in space of word-groups that have no comprehensible relation to each other when read consecutively in time. Instead of the instinctive and immediate reference of words and word-groups to the objects or events they symbolize and the construction of meaning from the sequence of these references, modern poetry asks its readers to suspend the process of individual reference temporarily until the entire pattern of internal references can be apprehended as a unity.[1]

Posterity again may destroy the effectiveness of this technique. It is now quite easy for habitual poetry readers to interpret poems of fragmentation in a superficial manner. They have learned how to make quick generalizations about the general area in which the apparently random images are working, and have thus learned how to avoid experiencing any of these images in depth.

A third method, one used by Donne, is the deliberate frustration of expectancy. This needs more explanation. When we hear any group of words we find ourselves unconsciously anticipating the nature of the

[1] Hardy and Westbrook, op. cit., p. 87.

following group. The phrase, 'The current epistemologies of academic philosophers', for example, arouses an expectation that the following words will be abstract, possibly polysyllabic, certainly unemotional, and clearly emanating from a speaker who has a highly 'educated' vocabulary. If the full sentence reads, 'The current epistemologies of academic philosophers are crap', we suffer a rude shock, even though we would have accepted the phrase 'altogether nonsensical', which means roughly the same thing in this context. This may be an absurd illustration, but to realize its importance one has only to think of the phrases and locutions one would not expect from radio announcers, stage Irishmen, commercial travellers, shy young women, or schoolteachers, to realize how firmly based this notion of expectancy is. This is not to say that our ideas of expectancy are sensible or logical, of course. They are often completely irrational. But they exist. And it is quite easy to utilize the reader's expectancy by surprising him with a quick change of tone or vocabulary. Consider the shifts in tone in this poem of Tony Connor's, the twelfth in his sequence, *For a Lost Girl*.

> I love you as I love the world,
>   turning away often to retch
> bile and bits I cannot hold
>
> in guts grown gross on the rich
>   diet of thirty years. Goddess—
> naked or clothed—wife, bitch,
>
> woman forever anonymous,
>   known only by your open thighs
> moist beneath mine in pitch darkness,
>
> will you be content with lies—
>   darling, my dear darling sweetheart—
> that I should love you less than this
>
> grave-ridden place in which I'm set—
>   down, amidst stinking histories,
> with all the wombs of earth to brat ?[1]

Expectancy also exists in terms of syntax. We can alter syntax in such a way as to frustrate the reader's expectations of what is to follow, and can also make parts of speech perform unexpected tricks. Thus we can

[1] Tony Connor, *With Love Somehow*, Oxford University Press, 1962, p. 64.

say, 'I walked through the lonely of the afternoon', where the reader is forced to give all his attention to the word lonely, as he has expected a noun descriptive of place and got the word 'of'. This means he must either insert, mentally, a word descriptive of place, or treat 'lonely' as if it were itself a place. Again, we can say, 'The was of everything is always now', or take an accepted phrase and alter it as in 'The quick and the fed', or 'In the beginning was the sword'. This particular use of obstruction is one familiar to readers of the poetry of George Barker, Dylan Thomas, and W. S. Graham, and, of course, e. e. cummings, whose poem *anyone lived in a pretty how town* we have already quoted.

Posterity, of course, will get used to some of these tricks and learn to treat them as superficially as it now treats such once valuable inventions as the Miltonic verse paragraph, the Donnian pun, and the Popeian ambiguity. There is, indeed, no obstructive technique that can be relied upon as being always effective. Therefore, the poet is always discovering new ones, and the consequence is that, in any period when poetry is really alive, the most lively poetry is likely to be accused of wilful obscurity, or distortion of the proper means of expression, or vulgarity, or something of that kind. All these accusations boil down to is the overall accusation that the poet is not doing what is expected of him. The poet, of course, is obliged to do the unexpected, for the expected is always immediately recognizable (having been anticipated, and tidily docketed in advance) and the recognized is rarely the perceived.

The greater part of our discussion so far has led us to the belief that the poem is less an explanation than a presentation; it becomes explanation only when we either separate its 'message' from its context, or indulge ourselves in a close critical analysis. As soon as it becomes, for us, explanation, however, it ceases to be presentation.

T. E. Hulme recognized this problem and in his essay on Romanticism and Classicism considered the importance and meaning of the word 'vital' as used by Coleridge.

> . . . Coleridge uses it in a perfectly definite and what I call dry sense. It is just this: A mechanical complexity is the sum of its parts. Put them side by side and you get the whole. Now vital or organic is merely a convenient metaphor for a complexity of a different kind, that in which the parts cannot be said to be elements as each one is modified by the other's presence, and each one to a certain extent is the whole. The leg of a chair by itself is still a leg. My leg by itself wouldn't be.
>
> Now the characteristic of the intellect is that it can only represent complexities of the mechanical kind. It can only make diagrams, and diagrams

are essentially things whose parts are separate from one another. The intellect always analyses—when there is a synthesis it is baffled. That is why the artists' work seems mysterious. The intellect can't represent it. This is a necessary consequence of the particular nature of the intellect and the purposes for which it is formed. It doesn't mean that your synthesis is ineffable, simply that it can't be definitely stated.

Now this is all worked out in Bergson, the central feature of his whole philosophy. It is all based on the clear conception of these vital complexities which he calls 'intensive', and the recognition of the fact that the intellect can only deal with the extensive multiplicity. To deal with the intensive you must use intuition.[1]

There are various corollaries to this. One of them is that if we regard life, which is to say the complexities of experience, as 'vital', in the way suggested by Hulme, then it must follow that the relationship of the intellect to experience is the same as that of the intellect to art. Consequently, any explanation of experience in intellectual terms must result in a distortion of reality. Hulme discusses this in an essay on Intensive Manifolds.

It is necessary then to show exactly in what way Bergson thinks that our ordinary methods of explanation distort reality. The process of explanation itself is generally quite an unconscious one. We explain things and it never strikes us to consider what we have done. We are as it were *inside* the process, and we cannot observe it, but you may get a hint of its nature by observing its effects. In any explanation you start off with certain phenomena, and you transform them into something else and say: 'This is what really happens'. There is something about this second state that satisfies the demands of your intellect, which makes you say: 'This is perfectly clear'. You have in your mind a model of what is clear and comprehensible, and the process of explanation consists in expressing all the phenomena of nature in terms of this model. I ought to say here that I am speaking not of ordinary explanation, but of explanation when it has gone to its greatest lengths, which is when it has worked itself out in any completed science like mechanics.[2]

Donald Davie, who also makes use of these two key passages of Hulme in his fine book, *Articulate Energy*, suggests that 'syntax is, on this showing, an extensive manifold; and since poetry must deal with intensive manifolds, it follows that in Hulme's view poetry has no use for syntax.'[3]

[1] T. E. Hulme, *Speculations*, Routledge and Kegan Paul, 1924, pp. 138–9.
[2] ibid., pp. 175–6. [3] Donald Davie, op. cit., p. 8.

This may well be the way Hulme's own mind worked, but it is not completely deduceable from the passages quoted, in that we can see, in these passages, indications that poetry is in some respects both an intensive and an extensive manifold.

It is obvious that poetry is intensive. Is it not however also true that poetry is an explanation as well ? We have suggested that this is not the case. When saying this we were, however, like Hulme, assuming that the process of explanation is purely intellectual, and therefore can concern itself only with complexities of a mechanical kind. If we agree with Hulme that we can discover the meaning of a word from its etymology—and this is very doubtful, for the meanings of words are created by usage as much as origin—then 'explanation', meaning the 'the opening out of things on a plain surface', must be alien to the synthesizing activity of poetry. But surely, in the description of explanation that we have quoted, the key sentence is 'You have in your mind a model of what is clear and comprehensible and the process of explanation consists in expressing all the phenomena of nature in terms of this model.' If this is the heart of the explanation process we must conclude that the exact nature of the process must vary in accordance with the model involved. If that model is a purely intellectual system of mechanical complexities, then Hulme's argument holds. If it is not purely intellectual, however : if it is, let us say, a system of animistic beliefs, a religious faith, a construction of superstitions, then, surely, the process of explanation may be vitalizing and enriching rather than otherwise. The primitive man who explains the heat of the day by saying that the Sun-God is angry has substituted for a perception of a physical discomfort the perception of a complex pseudo-human being. Nor can we argue that this process is not true explanation because the primitive man is not possessed of a model that is clear and comprehensible, for to him his model *is* clear and comprehensible; he can use it to explain vagaries of climate (which he does not understand) in terms of vagaries of human passion (which he does).

If we decide that explanation can be either intensive or extensive, and result in the construction of either organic or mechanical complexities, our only problem, when faced with an apparently explanatory activity, is to determine the nature of the model into whose terms the phenomena concerned are being translated. This touches directly on the problem of communication, for communication in language is itself a form of explanation, in that phenomena are being translated into words, and, frequently, in terms of a particular system of words.

The poem is therefore, to some extent, an explanation as well as a presentation, and we cannot continue to make the distinction between presentation and explanation, having realized that explanation itself need not be conducted in terms of intellectual analysis or definitions only. The poet, writing his poem, is aware that he is involved in an explanatory process, in that he is translating phenomena into words, and also relating new members of his construct-system to already existing members. So far as he is concerned the explanation is satisfactory if it has resulted in his 'getting things straight' as regards his own world of perception. Thus one aspect of the poem as an explanation is its purely private function for the individual composing the poem.

Words are, however, common property in that they are part of a system of counterparts which is regarded as having external reality by all observers. Therefore, in as much as language is being used, the poem is also public explanation, being a translation of phenomena in terms of a system which is public property.

Unfortunately, however, this system, while being public property, is subject to a massive degree of private manipulation. The dictionary may provide a key to the public aspect of the system, but cannot always reveal its private variations. Therefore, the degree to which the poem satisfies the reader as explanation is dependent upon the degree to which the reader shares, or can be made to share, the poet's own construct-system, or, at least, that part of it which is relevant for the poem in question.

No person, however, can completely share another person's construct-system. The most he can do is possess a construct-system that is disposed in a similar series of dynamic relationships. Thus, although one person's 'red' may differ from another person's, the general difference between 'red' and 'green' will be the same in both cases. If we accept this view we are forced back again upon Susanne Langer's view of poetry. It is a 'non-discursive symbolic form'.

This may, in the last resort, be true, but common sense tells us that words, no matter how we argue, are taken by the reader as referring to external realities. He will not accept statements which appear to him to be untrue in terms of those realities, however much he may intellectually concede the point that each person has a private perceptual world in which a statement that is false to him may appear to be correct. There is such a large measure of agreement between people as to the way in which words refer to inferred counterparts that this must be taken into account.

In fact, to the reader, the poem appears to be an arrangement of words indicating realities, which he can see in the context of his own perceptual world. Thus, provided that the poet and reader have both been conditioned by the same environment, and aware of the same systems of thought and belief, and are in general agreement over the nature of the externals they have inferred, the poem can operate on the informative level. T. E. Hulme, in his plan of writing a philosophical work 'having as its final object the destruction of the idea that the world has unity, or that anything can be described in words',[1] was being unreasonably idealistic.

We have not yet discovered, however, in what way the poem can be said to be an explanation of phenomena, except in so far as it is using words. It appears simply to re-present phenomena in words which have the same effect on the reader as those phenomena. This is not translating phenomena in terms of 'a model of what is clear and comprehensible', in that the model appears to the reader as if it were a mirror image of the phenomena themselves. It is here that we may bring primitive man back into the picture. A translation of phenomena into terms of human passions was for him an explanation. It is the same with the reader. The poem, by its structure, forces him to operate in a total fashion; it therefore relates the phenomena it presents to this total personality. Consequently the reader has the sense of phenomena being translated in terms of his own personal mode of perception, and thus in terms of his own construct-system. This construct-system is, to him, a 'clear and comprehensible' one—it is indeed the only thing that he experiences as clear and comprehensible, for it is his very criterion of clarity and intelligibility. Thus the poem is an explanation, although an intensive rather than an extensive manifold, because it translates phenomena into terms of the construct-system of each individual reader. Different readers will agree about the nature of what the poem 'puts across' only in so far as they agree about matters of emotion and intuition, though there is always likely to be a minimum agreement between members of the same culture.

We have now reached some kind of answer to our initial problem. It seems that poetry is not simply a morphology of feeling, not simply non-discursive symbolic form, but also a mode of explanation. It does not contain a 'message' as a mere control-factor, therefore, but also as an essential part of its meaning. We are returned to common sense. The poem that seems to be talking 'about' something is really talking about something, and explaining it. If we suggest that the manner of the

[1] T. E. Hulme, op. cit., p. xiv.

explanation may, in many cases, be more important than its informative aspect, we are saying no more than has been said of many explanations, whether in logic or chemistry. We are also suggesting, perhaps, that poetry is more frequently concerned to show us *how* we perceive than *what* we perceive, though no one, even in poetry, can ever really keep the two apart.

SEVEN Poetry, Magic, and Cult Art

I have suggested that a poem can be regarded as explanation, because it translates phenomena into terms of the reader's own construct-system—his model of whatever is most clear and intelligible. The reader who is involved in the experience of the poem is engaged, therefore, in the most thorough of explanatory procedures. If we accept this, then, how much of an explanation is the poem which translates phenomena into terms of a philosophic system ? This kind of explanation is, surely, an extensive rather than an intensive manifold, and thus is destructive of the complete participation by the reader in the poem concerned. If extensive and intensive manifolds co-exist in the poem, however, it may be that the poem itself presents yet another aspect of our manner of perception, for we continually destroy our perceptions of the vital nature of experience in order to provide ourselves with a working system of approximations which we can use to order and control our view of reality, from which viewpoint we can perceive further vital and organic complexities. The tension between the intensive and the extensive in the poem corresponds to a similar tension in our own methods of treating our perceptions.

Nevertheless, if the intellectual explanation (the extensive manifold) of the poem is in terms of a system which we cannot believe, our ability to participate in the poem is undermined. Consequently it may well be that the poem which hides its extensive manifold by couching it in words which are symbols (rather than allegorical references), to all but the cognoscenti, may succeed in solving the problem. Moreover, if the cognoscenti, the adherents of (let us say) neoplatonic thought, believe in the truth of that system, they will enrich it with emotional associations, and consequently regard the poem's 'message' as being vital rather than mechanical.

This is a tangled skein, and it is the more tangled because, in the reading of poetry, there are so very few stable elements. We must isolate one thread and try to draw it clear. Let us look at the problem of the Symbol.

In an earlier book[1] I defined the Poetic Symbol as a word which operates freely within its context, and whose 'meaning' is composed of the dynamic relationship of all its associations and implications. I suggested that as soon as a word with symbolic potentialities has those potentialities narrowed by its context so that only a proportion of them are allowed to be relevant, then it should be regarded as a 'sign', not a 'symbol'. Moreover if a word with symbolic potentiality is so closely bound by its context that it becomes simply a transcript 'standing for' something else, then the word must be described as a transcript, and symbolism has been replaced by allegory.

It was my contention in that book that the true symbol, the free holophrastic word with archetypal associations and power, enabled the reader to experience poetic perception the most intensely. This is not entirely true; some indication of the area in which the symbolic word has most relevance is usually required. When W. B. Yeats wrote,

> And what rough beast, its hour come round at last,
> Slouches towards Bethlehem to be born ?[2]

he did not limit the symbol of the beast by means of conceptual argument, but made it clear that it was a religious and mystical symbol by associating it with Bethlehem. We cannot therefore associate it with a shaggy dog, though we can associate it with dragons, the beast of the apocalypse, the minotaur, and so forth. From this we must deduce that the symbol usually has its general area of applicability indicated, but not its central definite 'meaning'. The symbol becomes a 'sign' when the area is restricted to two or three specific meanings, and becomes a 'transcript' when no area is indicated, only a defined significance.

This is an important qualification for otherwise one could maintain that the word 'bull' in the sentence 'The bull was angry' could be symbolic, whereas it could, equally well, be mere descriptive statement and not in any serious way holophrastic at all. The sentence, 'The bull was angry in the fields of Praise', however, could legitimately be regarded as implying the necessity of a symbolic reading, the area having been indicated in terms of spiritual and mythological qualities. Indeed, the symbol only succeeds when it is this kind of area that is suggested, for

[1] See Robin Skelton, *The Poetic Pattern*, Routledge and Kegan Paul, 1956.
[2] W. B. Yeats, *The Second Coming* in *Collected Poems*, Macmillan, 1950, p. 210.

only in this area are the associated ideas and meanings both powerful and pleromatic, and without definite intellectual contours. The symbol is a symbol because its associations are themselves symbolic; it is the centre of an ever-expanding universe, and this puts us in touch with a sensation of intense and vital organic movement, a sense of continual creation.

Once we read the symbolic poem as explanation in terms of a philo-sophic system, however, the symbol not only becomes a transcript, and thus loses its power to arouse sensations of continual creation, but also something we could perhaps usefully describe as Ikon, meaning an image which derives its significance from its attachment to a particular system. The transcript may be of an abstract quality such as truth in terms of persons or objects which are, in themselves, important. The Ikon, however, is not important in itself at all. An example would be the translation of the symbolic woman in terms, precisely, of the Virgin Mary. Only to adherents of Christianity, therefore, would this Ikon be symbolic, in the sense of having itself numerous symbolic associations.

This leads us directly to the problem of Cult Art. Within the cult the symbol can be read as an Ikon without losing its symbolic power. Outside it is likely to appear as a transcript of an arbitrary notion. To what extent is Cult Art an evasion of artistic problems, and to what extent is it simply an ordinary poetic method developed in terms of a culture existing within the confines of the larger culture? If Cult Art is simply describable as such because the culture upon which it is based is one involving a small number of people rather than a large, is it not possible that it may be able to probe more deeply than other art, because its audience, being smaller, contains fewer serious differences of interpretive habits?

We have arrived now at a central problem of communication, and it may be helpful to argue from a particular example. Blake's poem, *The Little Girl Lost*, conveys to the vast majority of readers a story about a little girl, aged seven, who was lost in the desert, and, because of her innocence, protected and loved by the wild beasts. The opening two verses of the poem are taken as being a prophecy that the earth will, eventually, wake from its sloth and find God, when the lion will lie down with the lamb. Those readers, however, who have read more of Blake will realize that this poem indicates the viewpoint of the unfallen soul, and regard the poem as having a deep significance as a picture of Eden (or something of the kind). The expert, however, will tell us that the story is based upon Blake's understanding of neoplatonic thought, and that it concerns the 'descent of the soul into generation', and will interpret even the most straightforward lines in an allegorical fashion. Kathleen Raine, for example, says of the lines,

> Sweet sleep, come to me
> Underneath this tree.

The apparent naivety of the lines could not be more misleading: they are fraught with condensed traditional symbolic meaning. The symbol of the Tree in Blake signifies always the natural universe, the vegetated condition of generation. . . .[1]

Only a few readers would understand the poem in this way for it is, on the surface, a very simple, and quite touching story.

> In futurity
> I prophetic see
> That the earth from sleep
> (Grave the sentence deep)

> Shall arise and seek
> For her maker meek;
> And the desart wild
> Become a garden mild.

> In the southern clime,
> Where the summer's prime
> Never fades away,
> Lovely Lyca lay.

> Seven summers old
> Lovely Lyca told;
> She had wander'd long
> Hearing wild birds' song.

> 'Sweet sleep, come to me
> Underneath this tree.
> Do father, mother weep,
> Where can Lyca sleep?

[1] Kathleen Raine, 'The Little Girl Lost and Found and The Lapsed Soul' in *The Divine Vision, Studies in the Poetry and Art of William Blake*, Gollancz, 1957, pp. 28–9.

Lost in desart wild
Is your little child.
How can Lyca sleep
If her mother weep ?

If her heart does ake
Then let Lyca wake;
If my mother sleep,
Lyca shall not weep.

Frowning, frowning night,
O'er this desart bright
Let thy moon arise
While I close my eyes.'

Sleeping Lyca lay
While the beasts of prey,
Come from caverns deep,
View'd the maid asleep.

The kingly lion stood
And the virgin view'd,
Then he gambol'd round
O'er the hallow'd ground.

Leopards, tygers, play
Round her as she lay,
While the lion old
Bow'd his mane of gold

And her bosom lick,
And upon her neck
From his eyes of flame
Ruby tears there came;

While the lioness
Loos'd her slender dress
And naked they convey'd
To caves the sleeping maid.

Here is a case of the poem conveying a quite different meaning and kind of meaning to the majority of its readers than to a specially informed minority. It is indisputable that the minority poem has more of a 'message', and is a more interesting object, but which is the true 'poem'? The 'message' is, clearly, not operating here as a control-factor. It is the story, the sequential structure, which presents a definite episode that gives us the unity of the poem. Thus the majority poem does not give a less intense feeling of a completed pattern than the minority poem, as is sometimes the case. Nevertheless, if we decide that the poem is written, perhaps unconsciously, for the ideal reader, then we must suppose that the ideal reader is the one who is as informed as the poet himself about the various beliefs and systems underlying the poem. It is however unreasonable to say that because the poet writes for a particular audience, then that audience is the only one fitted to read the poem. In any case, the poet while writing, rarely has the communicative aspect of the poem in the forefront of his mind. He simply tries, as I. A. Richards has pointed out, to get the work 'right'.

> To make the work 'embody', accord with, and represent the precise experience upon which its value depends is his major preoccupation, in difficult cases an overmastering preoccupation, and the dissipation of attention which would be involved if he considered the communicative side as a separate issue would be fatal in most serious work. He cannot stop to consider how the public or even how especially well qualified sections of the public may like it or respond to it. He is wise, therefore, to keep all such considerations out of mind altogether.[1]

On the other hand, the poet, when deciding whether or not to publish his verses, does think of the communicative aspect of his work, and some didactic poets are concerned with communication almost from the beginning. Nevertheless, the poet's procedure

> does, in the majority of instances, make the communicative efficacy of his work correspond with his own satisfaction and sense of its rightness. This may be due merely to his normality, or it may be due to unavowed motives. The first suggestion is the more plausible. In any case it is certain that no mere careful study of communicative possibilities, together with any desire to communicate, however intense, is ever sufficient without close natural correspondence between the poet's impulses and possible impulses in his reader. All supremely successful communication involves this correspondence, and no planning can take its place.[2]

[1] I. A. Richards, *Principles of Literary Criticism*, Routledge and Kegan Paul, 1924, pp. 26–7.
[2] ibid., p. 29.

Let us imagine that a poet has written a poem which, to him, has various 'echoes' of other poems which enrich his own, and which also includes, as a part of its structure, a philosophic message. Let us then suppose that, because the structure of the poem accurately parallels the nature of the perceptual process, and because all the images used are ones which can easily affect everyone living in his own country and speaking his own language, the poem is widely read and enjoyed. We then will get, let us say, some thousands of people enjoying the poem as a certain experience with one message, a fewer number, some hundred perhaps, appreciating also the 'echoes', and thus enjoying a more complex structure, and maybe only twenty or thirty people understanding the presence of a definite philosophic message. Now, the more complex the structure that is perceived, the more difficult it is to be completely participant in the poem. Thus we reach the paradox that the most informed reader of the poem may be incapable of experiencing it as an act of perception to the same degree as the least informed reader.

Nevertheless, by writing a poem which is, in some sort, an example of Cult Art, the poet has been able to utilize the special awarenesses of some of his readers, in order to make the poem more complex, rich, and meaningful. Had he not used references to other poems and to an existing philosophical system, he would have had to present these aspects of his perception at greater length, and therefore distort and alter the pattern. Moreover, by using an allusive technique, he has incorporated into his perceptual structure the sensation of man's relationship to remembered art-experience, and to the activity of the systematizing intellect. Thus, Cult Art can, in some ways, be richer and more profound than art which is composed entirely in terms of a wide culture.

It is obviously unfair, however, to say that the minority poem is, in this case, the only true poem. It is simply a different one. Moreover, there are always disadvantages in treating the poem as if it has only one identity, for such a treatment denies the nature of human perception. The poem is what it is for each reader, and that is one of the most important aspects of its communicative or explanatory quality.

We have now reached a point where it is important to observe the relationship of the poem with society from a slightly different angle. There is a generally accepted belief that the minority poem is the true poem, and that only the informed reader has the right to express an opinion about a poem's success or failure. This feeling is largely a product of academicism. The academic student of literature is only different from the casual poetry reader in one respect. He has more information. Like the casual reader, he insists that his is the real poem, but can back up his statement, not with the remark that 'This is my taste', but with the assertion, 'This is my knowledge.' He can show the casual reader that his poem is more complex than the majority poem. He cannot, however, show that it is more of a poem, a more intense perception. Indeed, it often is a less intense perception, because a more purely intellectual one. The academic is inclined to indulge himself in what Richards describes as 'the substitution of an intellectual formula for a work of art'. Very frequently, because the minority poem differs from the majority poem largely in its greater intellectual complexity, the teacher of poetry finds himself emphasizing the extensive manifold of the poem, and treating it (for perfectly good reasons) as a vehicle for a 'message'. Once he has done this, the poem becomes dependent for its validity upon the validity of the message which has been extracted. If, as is often the case, this 'message' has been more clearly delivered by a psychologist, philosopher, or mystic, then the poem ceases to be of any real importance, except as music. Thousands of theses upon the 'Theme of X in the Poetry of Y', or 'The influence of the philosophy of A upon the poetry of B' testify to the continual academic treatment of poems as vehicles rather than as organisms.

This would not, perhaps, matter very much, were it not that the main influences upon the attitude of the community towards poetry are controlled by people who have suffered this training. Consequently we find that poetry is popularly regarded as 'difficult' or 'obscure' simply because the majority are unable to provide themselves with the kind of substitute poem or poem-as-vehicle which their mentors have told them is the only real poem. Sometimes a poet can overcome this difficulty. The poetry of Dylan Thomas is widely read today because of its sheer perceptual exuberance, and because the terms in which he was discussed after his death were such as to imply that he was a drunk singer of genius, and not that horrid creature an 'intellectual'.

In the adulation of Dylan Thomas there is also another element. He has, in the popular myth of his life and death, not only the advantage of not being an 'intellectual', but the greater advantage of being a dyonisiac and possessed figure. No matter how often we recall the sober and industrious lives of so many poets, we cannot ever escape the notion that the poet's authority stems from his being 'possessed' by the Muse. Indeed, one aspect of the whole notion of Cult Art is related to the idea of poet as Priest, as Keeper of the Sacred Texts. We must set the notion of poetry as magic alongside that of poetry as explanation and explore the social function of poetry, and the nature of its communicative process farther.

Let us notice first of all that there is a magical element in all language, and also that the majority of words are, in a more precise fashion than we have already suggested, indications, not of externals, but of private creations by the individual.

The basic assumptions of magic are two-fold. First, that the name is inseparable from the object, and that the speaking of the name causes the object to exist, in that a mental event is as real as anything we know. Thus the spoken word is a creation of the identity of which that word is a central part. Language is itself a way of controlling reality. As Professor Toshihiko Izutsu has said,

> To the mind of early man it is not some particular words, not particular sentences that are dangerous, but . . . every word, every sentence, in short, all speaking is awful and sacred. There is, strictly speaking, no trivial word. For the ancients as well as for the primitives, to speak, i.e. to utter speech sounds, to pronounce the names of things, means something not to be made light of. For the speech, once uttered from the mouth, calls forth some hidden force from the—seemingly—most ordinary and innocent objects and persons, powerfully influences the course of natural and human events, and, in many cases, may give entrance to the peril. To state or declare something to be so and so means at once to make the object actually so and so. In Hebrew, for instance, the causative form of the verb (the so-called Hiphil form) does not distinguish between declaring and making.[1]

The result of this belief was that wars were carried on as much in terms of words as swords. Indeed, if a battle was lost, it was often believed that the magician-poet of one side had been bested by the magician-poet of the other, and in certain cases disputes were decided by a comparative show of force, not in terms of armament, but in terms of oratory. It is amusing to see in this the origin of the debate, in which it is the 'power' of the words, as opposed to their rational qualities, that usually determines the result.

Now, today, we realize that we understand in terms of patterns, of *gestalten*, and that the magical formula or spell gave its speaker a sense of 'understanding' in that it arranged the situation it described into a pattern. It is not a big step from the belief that one understands a

---

[1] Toshihiko Izutsu, *Language and Magic*, The Keio Institute of Philological Studies, Tokyo, 1956, p. 25.

situation to the feeling that one is in control of it. 'To mean something by means of speech', said Walter Porzig, 'is no other than a weakened form of the intention to bind it magically.'

There is, however, another assumption of magic that is important. If words are powerful, the more intensity they are given, the more 'life' that is given to them by the speaker, the more powerful they become. Until a word is spoken, it has no power, for there is no breath, no spirit, no mana in it. 'It is in the breath', says Professor Izutsu, 'that the main virtue of all verbal magic is believed to reside. The words, so long as it is not actually pronounced, must of necessity remain slumbering and inactive; only when carried by the breath can it become efficacious.'[1] Indeed, the word can only operate magically when it is pronounced with 'strong breath'—that is to say when it is pronounced with intention.

In this belief we can see the origin of emphatic verse rhythms, and also the irrational instinctive belief that underlies the raising of the voice in argument, or at moments when a person is emotionally keyed up to the necessity to convince or dominate. It also explains the use of particular styles of speech by preachers and orators; the sing-song style is simply vestigial magic.

So far we have said nothing that is not already well known; there are, however, new deductions to be made in the light of our recent discussions on communication. Let us first of all notice that the identification of speaker with maker is one that is not only sensible to those who believe in the Sense-datum Theory, but also to ordinary people, unacquainted with the work of psychologists and philosophers.

The facts of the case are simple. Because, to us, at a deep level, words are the inward natures of objects, every time we hear a word we presume the existence of an object or pseudo-object which has the word as its 'name'. We are forced into this position by our regarding all the constructs of our private world as having reference to some system of externals. We do this because we must observe them as if we were separate from them in order to place them into manipulatable patterns. We cannot create a manipulatable pattern if the manipulator himself is part of it. We cannot believe that the subject and object, the creator and the creation, the mover and the moved, the explicator and the explanation, can be one. Consequently, whenever we hear a word, we infer an external to correspond with it. If I say, 'Blarinek dariter fluckly', though you may dismiss it as meaningless gibberish, you will still find

[1] ibid., p. 27.

yourselves uneasily wondering what it *might* mean. Professor Izutsu, again, has something to say about this:

> ... whenever a name-word is uttered in the absence of the object it tends to make the hearer *think* or *feel* as if he were in the presence of the object; in other words, by making the object mentally present, it tends to cause the hallucination that the thing-meant, whatever that may be, really existed. Since our early experience with language almost always warranted the actual existence of anything whatsoever named by a word, we have, it would seem, fallen unwittingly into the bad habit of expecting a substantival entity to exist whenever we hear a general word uttered.[1]

It is certainly true that, whenever a small child utters a sound that has any resemblance to a word, the fond parents inform it that it is referring to some object or need (often puzzling the child, who was simply practicing making noises). Moreover quite soon the child discovers that noises affect external realities, and thus comes to regard the noises in the magical fashion we have described. Professor Izutsu remarks,

> Besides, from the viewpoint of the traditional ontology which recognizes *potentia* as a special manner of existing as distinguished from *actus*, there is certainly a sense in which there is no essential difference between the idea of the object X existing and the idea pure and simple of the object X, for, as Kant emphasized in his criticism of the ontological argument, it is impossible to represent an object without attributing to it a certain amount of existence, be it that of a mere possible. This means that by the very fact of being represented, the object X has already gained some kind of existence, for it does exist at least as a mere possible. And the possible existence of an object once posited, it is but an easy step from there to our erecting that possible object into a real object. A huge number of such pseudo-entities are thus generated; in this way the Platonic realm of Ideas comes to being.[2]

Thus we create a whole range of constructs which are not in any real sense referential to anything external. The language system forces us, too, into the creation of pseudo-entities. Izutsu refers to Bloomfield as pointing out that

> *fire*, according to physicists, is not a thing but rather an action or process, and is therefore more appropriately to be described by the verb *burn* than the noun *fire*. But no sooner have we begun to say, for example, 'the fire burns and gives out light and heat', than we fall into the danger of reading into nature bogus entities capable of performing miraculous actions: thus in the case here

[1] ibid., p. 66.   [2] ibid., p. 66.

envisaged a self-subsistent entity *fire* becomes postulated and is made to perform some kind of action called *burning* and to produce, furthermore, other substances named *light* and *heat*.[1]

Syntactical forms can create pseudo-entities quite easily. We say that this pillar box is red, and find ourselves postulating the existence of redness as a quality of an external. In fact we should say, as Izutsu suggests in other terms, 'This pillar box reds me', as the colour is an attribute not of the pillar box but of ourselves. An exhaustive study of the relationship of language-systems to meanings reveals that one might go so far as to say that speech creates meanings and objects continually, and that a high proportion of all words refer to pseudo-entities.

I have said that ordinary people unacquainted with psychology, linguistics, or philosophy, realize that the speaker is a maker. This is clear once we listen to any discussion or disagreement. An assertion that X is Y, where Y is pseudo-entity, is often countered by the statement that X is Z, and followed by the solution X is Y *to me*, though it may appear to be Z *to you*. This is the case with all words denoting qualities, particularly those denoting features of character, shades of colour, intensities of sound, accuracies of description, and truth or falsity. Moreover, in any company you will hear assertive statements made in the form 'I say', or 'I think', or 'I believe', which are clearly understood as meaning 'In my world of perception, which may be different from yours, this is the case.' People, indeed, are keenly aware that each speaker makes his own reality, and also that the 'stronger the breath' the more real the statement (to the speaker, at least). They are also aware of the deliberate magical activity of the speaker; a common retort is 'You say that because you wish it were true', or, more shortly, 'That's what *you* say.'

Most people are more aware than one might suppose that 'the constitution of our primary world of reality depends in large measure upon the structural patterns of our language' and that, frequently, 'What common sense believes to be the concrete, objective reality proves, upon a closer inspection, to be largely a product of our linguistic habits.'

They would not, of course, use these words. They would rather say, 'That's one way of putting it, I suppose' (meaning 'That is one way of ordering reality, one way of making'), or 'I see it differently', where 'see' really means 'shape'. They say, 'What do you make of it?' when asking for an explanation, and they say of a man's actions, 'It speaks well for

[1] ibid., p. 94.

him that he did that.' They connect force of emphasis with physical transmission and tell us that 'He spoke out against it' and they attach the idea of speech to the notion of spirit. 'Will you take my word for it ?' 'I'll accept your word, of course.' 'Give me your word.' These are all examples from English vernacular, for we are, after all, discussing English poetry and our own community, but even more impressive examples can be found in other languages.

All this leads us to the view that people are aware of the making aspect of language, believe instinctively in language as magic, and are affected by the notion of verbal emphasis as magical power.

If this is the case, we can explain many aspects of poetry (and of the arts generally) in its relationship to the community, and thus in relationship to the idea of communication. First of all let us observe that the poem is obviously a highly organized form of speech and that whenever we see an example of complex organization we presume intention behind it. We say, 'It cannot be accidental', and add, 'There must be a purpose.' Moreover poetry, by its indication (explicit or implicit) of emotion and its emphatic use of rhythm, gives the impression that the speaker of the poem is speaking with magical power. Therefore what the poem 'means' is what the powerful speaker intends to control. If we assent to a poem, and allow ourselves to participate in it, to share its experience, we are assenting to its intentions. It thus becomes important to know what it means. The common distrust of obscurity in modern poetry and art is simply the fear of hidden meanings which might be assented to unwittingly, because of the strong 'personality' of the art-object. This can be seen clearly in the case of people who don't 'understand' abstract painting, and who say they don't like it. Tell them that there is nothing to understand—that they must simply enjoy the colours, forms, and spaces, and whatever else they feel inclined—and they frequently become devotees.

If it is important to know what a poem means, which is to say what objects it is controlling, and in what way it is manipulating them, then the view that the minority poem of the cognoscenti is a truer poem than the poem of the majority is easily explained. The minority poem almost invariably controls more objects, and is therefore more powerful and regarded as more of a poem. The didactic element in poetry—its references to facts that are important in themselves, and its judgements in terms of pseudo-entities—is therefore an appeal to the magically minded. It may seem odd to say this when it is the rationalist who most strongly objects to 'meaningless' poetry, and who demands a strong informative content, but it is none the less the case. Moreover, it is the two separate strands of magical belief—that in words as the inner natures of things, and that in the power of the intensive utterance—which combine as extensive and intensive manifolds in the poem which is in any way both didactic and reflexive. The failure of much didactic poetry lies simply in its tendency to omit a full presentation of a personality deeply involved in the poem's intentions, and the failure of much purely reflexive poetry lies in its lacking any indication of an intention to affect reality; it is simply a presentation of the control of the controlling mechanism, and thus lacks any impression, for most readers, of man's impulse towards action. It is poetry only for those to whom self-analysis is a purposive activity rather than an introspective indulgence.

We have now reached the point where we can suggest that the referential or didactic element in poetry presents a magical view of reality. Without any clear didactic element the poem cannot appear to be controlling or patterning a reality external to the reader, and therefore cannot reflect adequately the universal human habit of ordering inferred externals in order to control and understand them. The presence in the poem of a semblance of reference or message or argument (and, as we have seen, abstract ideas are pseudo-entities, and felt as objects to a considerable degree) is not sufficient, for the poem must reflect accurately the existence of man in a world that is composed not only of private perceptual systems, but of beliefs about external counterparts of those systems. Thus the 'aboutness' of poetry, its extensive manifold, is an integral part of its structure.

We are here, however, faced with a difficulty. It has often been maintained that poetry is a form of magic. Certainly, in primitive societies, poetry was always thus regarded, and verbal magic was always made in what we would regard as 'poetry'. It is, however, illogical to assume because the corpus of poetry includes magic that poetry *is* magic. We have shown that there is much magic in our approach to language, admittedly, but we have not agreed that magic is, in fact, able to affect reality in the way in which truly magic-dominated societies believed. There may be many traces of magical thinking in our attitude to the world we live in, but our attitudes are affected by our conscious as well as our unconscious beliefs, and few people today would admit to believing in 'magic', as such. This being so, as poetry is what it is to the community in which it finds itself and has no absolute existence of its own, we cannot but doubt that poetry, in as far as it is consciously experienced, is experienced as magic.

Of course, we can answer this doubt quite easily by suggesting that a poem is like an iceberg; the greater part of it is under water. Most of its elements are experienced intuitively rather than intellectually. May it not be true that the magical nature of poetry also 'comes across' in this submarine fashion ?

The answer is not entirely wrong. We do experience a sense of the poem as a magical controlling of reality. We do derive a feeling of spiritual power from the force of the rhythm and the sonority of the music. And in writing the poem, the poet does feel that he is manipulating realities, getting them straight, as well as performing a true act of creation. Moreover, so great is our instinctive belief in the poem as a message or conjuration delivered with the whole spiritual force of the speaker, that we habitually speak of what 'X says' or 'Y says', although we know full well that every poem is, to some extent, a dramatic monologue, and spoken by a fictional person created (perhaps unconsciously) to perceive and speak from a certain viewpoint, which may or may not be closely allied to the poet's own.

Nevertheless, the doubt remains, for we can set against this picture of the situation another one. Is it not true that, while a real believer in magic is convinced that a spell can affect external reality, the poem clearly suggests, over and over again, the subjective nature of the universe, and thus replies to the magician, 'You can affect only the ordering of your own construct-system' ? Belief in magic depends upon belief in an external world; words are the essential natures of real objects, and there can be no word without a real object. Poetry may treat words in this fashion, but it also, by its use of metaphor, and by its use of the 'scientifically' incredible, forces us to acknowledge that words create the objects. Consequently it asserts the primacy of the speaker, and undermines the magician's view that language is a means of controlling an already totally existent world exterior to himself. It could be said that the poet is, however, a magician in that he creates new realities from existing ones, which is a form of magically affecting an existing situation. He, like the mythical magician, can turn people to stones, or, like Faustus, grow antlers upon the brow of a fool. It is here, however, that our control factor again becomes important, for the 'message' of the poem is most usually explicable in terms of ordinary rationality, and most frequently includes at least a semblance of argument.

Let us take the argumentative element first. Magic is not argumentative. Where there is magic there is assertion and sometimes deduction, but never, within the one charm or spell, counter-assertion and counter-deduction. There can be no oppositions or the spell would cancel itself out, and there is no need for intellectual argument, in that manic assertion is regarded as being more powerful than reason or logic. Any deductions the spell makes are false deductions, being rather in the form 'let X cause Y' than the form 'Y follows inevitably and in all cases from X.' Moreover, the spell or charm rarely presents the evil it is attempting to cure, nor the good it is attempting to change, in verbal detail. The wax figure, the hair of the person, or simply the name of the person, may be used as objects of the spell's activity, but the existing attributes of the object are never elaborated upon, for this would be to set up an opposition to the spell's success. The poem, however, presents, not the alteration of the situation, but the situation as it is. No sensible magician would, in order to charm a girl to his bed, present a verbal pattern of her beauty and his despair; he would rather present a pattern of his success and her subjection. No magician, wishing to alter the times he lived in, would write a satire; he would compose an idyll. The magical poem, indeed, is an attack upon a situation understood rather than stated, and its disposition of references to externals is the heart of its structure. Poetry, on the other hand, is the presentation of the situation in order that we may feel ourselves to be in control of it, and after the poem attack it by (presumably) other means. In this respect poetry, in so far as it is an action upon events, is unlike the magic spell.

Poetry may be more like an invocation or incantation, of course, a raising up of spirits in order to control them. Here, its presentation of situation is directly analogous to magical activity. The situation is presented in the form of a carefully arranged pattern. The speaker uses a properly emphatic rhythm, a properly resonant tone. The result is the recreation of an act of perception, which we then feel able to understand and control. This is clearly a more serious argument, for we can safely say of any poem, whatever it involves, that it presents a situation in a pattern, and that it is feasible to suppose that the poet wrote it in order to 'get things straight'. Surely poetry, if not a kind of magic spell, is a kind of magical incantation.

Here again, however, there is a difficulty. The magical invocation must be seen as involving a subject and an object. The magician can only conjure up the presence of forces which he regards as being external to himself; he cannot be himself a part of the pattern he dominates. Thus, if we are to regard a poem as a magical conjuration of this kind, we must assume the existence of a Super-Speaker who is able to conjure up the actual speaker of the poem. We must, in other words, regard the I of the poem as a fiction separate from the personality of the perceiver. This we can easily manage. Each poem is, after all, to some extent a dramatic monologue, as we have said. We can, therefore, say that poetry is magical; we can say this, as long as we do not, in reading the poem, become at one with its act of perception, for if we do this we are regarding the poem as subject, not object. The whole endeavour of the poem, however, is to involve us in this way. We must experience the pattern and not only look at it from the outside. Thus, though the poet may be at one level a magician, the poem, when it is read more than superficially, is, to the reader, something other than magic. It is at once, for the reader, the perception of a pattern, and perception by means of the pattern, and the sense of control is as much in terms of the perceiver as of the perceived.

Let us gather the threads together. It is clear that magical belief and magical methods are involved in the poetic process for both reader and writer. A great part of the poem's effect depends upon the reader's having a magical attitude to language. Nevertheless, these aspects of the poetic experience are balanced by others. The poem is usually unlike a magical spell in that it makes use of intellectual conflicts, and contains its own pattern of oppositions rather than existing in a dynamic relationship with an 'understood' reality. It is unlike a spell, too, in that its 'message' is frequently dependent for its intellectual validity upon beliefs opposed to magical ones, and in that it makes use of rational, as well as imaginative, procedures and progressions. It is unlike an incantation or conjuration, too, in that the perceiver is part of the created pattern, and the reader is required not only to observe that perceiver, but to experience him subjectively. In other words, magic is invariably in terms of extensive manifolds of one kind or another; poetry also makes use of intensive manifolds. The only argument against this view that remains is that the reader is himself the 'object' of the spell, or magical activity, and that his involvement in the act of perception of the poem is simply his assent to the magical act, his being successfully 'bewitched'. This is certainly one aspect of the reader's experience, as we have seen. There is however the opposed aspect: he is not only made to feel in control as well as controlled, but able to understand as well as suffer the mechanism which has resulted in this twin feeling. He can safely be said to be in a dual relationship with the poem. As Dewey has pointed out, 'In short, art, in its form, unites the very same relation of doing and undergoing, outgoing and incoming energy, that makes an experience to be an experience.'[1]

[1] John Dewey, op. cit., p. 48.

In examining poetry and magic we have, indeed, again reached a realization of poetry as 'mutual organization of the factors of both action and reception into one another.' We might add to this that, as far as magic is concerned, poetry makes use of instinctive magical attitudes, and puts them accurately in place in its presentation of the structure of perception, revealing at once their power and their limitations.

There is, however, another aspect of magic which needs discussion. Magic has been discussed in terms purely of isolated verbal acts; underlying these acts, and justifying them, is a system of belief in the nature of causality, which leads inevitably to a certain method of thinking. If we assume that magic is the greatest causal power that exists, and if we suppose that magical spells and incantations do alter external reality, then we must answer the question, 'How or Why does this happen?' in magical terms. Let us take the case of Magician A whose spell does not work. On being taxed with this, he simply replies that it has not worked because another Magician, Y, has been opposing him. The rains have not fallen because of some malign influence, some sin in the tribe. Search out the sinner. Again, if asked why plague visited the village, the witch-doctor reports that bad magic, or a malign spiritual influence has been responsible. There is no disproving this statement. A scientist may refer to bacilli, or climatic conditions, or any one of a hundred causes, but the witch-doctor can come back with the retort, 'Yes, but why did the bacilli come here?' The argument can never reach a conclusion. Once posit spiritual powers as causes within the framework of a good-bad view of existence, and what Professor Max Gluckmann has called Witchcraft Thinking is inevitable.

We need not laugh at the African tribesman for thinking in these terms. We ourselves indulge in witchcraft thinking not infrequently. In Soviet Russia the explanation of disorder tends to be in terms of 'reactionary forces'. In Nazi Germany the explanation was in terms of the Jews. In America 'Communism' is the opposing magical influence. Nor is witchcraft thinking absent from religion. 'Sins' are responsible for all kinds of suffering. Prayers and rituals are used magically to combat the forces of evil. Hymns and prayers are often in the form of magical spells and incantations, and regarded magically. Some hymns are, of course, poetry turned to magic formulae by environmental influence and specific emphases, the occasion distorting the structure. Some hymns (and some spells and charms) though written with a strictly magical purpose also turn out, when abstracted from their native ritualistic environment, to be poetry, of course. Magical verbal patterns, however, are, usually, in so far as they are efficient in terms of magical belief and practice, weak as poetry. Any reader of magical spells and incantations will discover that there is something missing in their structures that is present in good poetry.

We have, by examining magic and poetry from a different viewpoint, seen some of the things that magic lacks. Our concern now is with the system of witchcraft thinking that underlies the practice of magic, and also many religious and political formulations. Witchcraft thinking is a form of explanation. Phenomena have been translated in terms of a 'model' which the believer finds clear and intelligible because it is unassailable and unanswerable. Moreover it is absolute. It cannot be altered by the individual in any way. It is, as a system, complete. Admittedly it is theoretically possible for one side in the struggle to totally defeat the other but this is not a serious contention on the part of the witchcraft thinkers. 'Reaction' and 'Communism' are intellectual or spiritual forces and eternal. 'Reaction' will always exist, as long as the idea of 'Progress' exists: 'Communism' will always remain because it can mean anything that is against the Establishment. 'Communism' in South Africa is simply a word to cover any liberal tendency, any movement against the Apartheid State.

This absolute and unchangeable aspect of the system in terms of which things must be explained is precisely the point at which poetry attacks witchcraft thinking. Poetry 'explains' in terms of the reader's own construct-system. It refers all its judgements to the subjective experience of the human psyche. Now, one thing every person knows is that the private construct-system is not an absolute. It alters its dispositions daily, and it alters them as the poem itself proceeds. Consequently, the poem presents phenomena in terms of a participant perceiver, and suggests that there is no absolute system of forces in terms of which every person can describe the operations of causality.

This may be the tendency of poetry as a structure, but it is not, necessarily, the tendency of the particular poem with a particular 'message'. We can easily find poems whose 'messages' are couched in witchcraft thinking. There are propagandist poems which are also good poems, and there are religious poems (as opposed to spells) that are among the greatest we have, although their judgements are (as regards the 'message') in witchcraft terms.

It is here that we see again the extraordinary dynamic comprehensiveness of the poetic method. Poetry as structure takes one attitude; poetry as message takes another. This we can observe, not only in terms of the witchcraft situation, but also in terms of the approach to history, dogma, time, morality, and so forth.

We have said that poetry presents an act of perception by the total personality in a fashion that is precisely true to the nature of the perceptual process. We have further suggested that a poem is a person, and demands from the reader an involvement in the activity of the I of the poem. Having emphasized this, we then discovered that the 'message', the didactic element, of the poem was one means of controlling the pattern and giving it shape, as well as a means of giving the reader a sense of understanding and controlling, not only the perceptual process, but also the objects of perception. The 'message' forces the reader not only to see the true nature of perception, but also to balance this against his ordinary assumptions and beliefs about the perceived world. We can now add to this a further function of 'meaning'. It can bring us sharply up against the difference between the experience and the inference, the reality and the approximation, the maximal and the minimal use of our inward understanding of life. Meaning may be, ultimately, of less importance than structure, but meaning is the means by which the importance of the structure can be estimated. Meaning makes the poem an act upon the community in a new way. It forces value judgements upon the reader. And, let us remember, if the poem is to present the perceptual process accurately, it must also involve the reader in judgement activities. It must also, however, make clear just how these judgement activities operate; judgement, like emotional involvement, must be seen in the context of a complex and dynamic whole, no part of which can be ignored without risk. Poetry, by continually drawing attention to the complex organization of perceptual procedures, and to the system of tensions and balances in which any 'message' or 'meaning' invariably exists, does itself present a kind of judgement of all other and more approximate modes of communication and decision. It is not only the presentation and explanation of acts of perception; it is also a directive which lies at the very heart of the liberal and humanist tradition.

EIGHT The Truth of Poetry

We have, to some extent, been looking at values all along, and this chapter must be concerned less with developing new ideas than with re-stating and systematizing ideas that have already been expressed.

First of all, let us consider poetry as an ethic. This is easy enough. If we accept the view that poetry is constantly emphasizing the subjective nature of the universe, and indicating that any action we take must be seen as in the context of our individual worlds of perception, rather than in the context of a world of inferred externals, we arrive at the conclusion that it is impossible to judge the 'rightness' or 'wrongness' of any action. Good and bad are purely relative terms. We cannot know the real context of any action, as we cannot completely share the perceptual world of any other creature. Thus poetry echoes the biblical dictum 'judge not', and exposes rules of conduct and laws as being working systems rather than absolute truths.

We cannot, however, get away with a completely anarchic view of morality, for there is another aspect of poetry which suggests the existence of a moral principle which should guide our conduct. Poetry is, all the time, concerned to establish the wonderful complexity of human nature, and is concerned with putting each reader into a sympathetic relationship with people. There is an assumption that, although each person may have a different world of perception, everyone creates his world of perception in a similar manner, and is moved by similar necessities. Poetry forces us to share the life of others at the deepest possible levels. There is an attempt to experience life in a total fashion, to involve oneself in the business of life in order (presumably) to come at some external truth. Pierre Emmanuel, speaking of the way in which he, as a poet, involves himself in a participant relationship with the world he knows by means of images, wrote:

> What I do know from experience is that thinking in images sets at stake, both physically and mentally, the whole hierarchy of being: it is not detached from the object, but committed in concrete existence, and step by step includes the

117

universe. And thereby, man *thinks in concord* with the world which surrounds him, he is both part and whole.[1]

John Dewey has emphasized this point.

> The moments when the creature is both most alive and most composed and concentrated are those of fullest intercourse with the environment, in which sensuous material and relations are most completely merged. Art would not amplify experience if it withdrew the self into the self nor would the experience that results from such retirement be expressive.[2]

Thus, we cannot take a solipsist view of life if we are to accept the values of poetry. We must, however, recognize that, as Pierre Emmanuel has said,

> Each of us carries within him the countenance of his God: or, to use terms more easily grasped by those who believe in God without knowing it, the universal form of man. Our common basis of existence is also our supreme end. Whoever tries to diminish me, to disfigure me in such a way that I become ashamed of what I am, outrages human nature in me, the countenance which we have in common: he disfigures himself at the same time, which is really what he wants to do, whether he is aware of it or not.[3]

Poetry, indeed, teaches reverence for the individual. While we cannot judge the rightness or wrongness of his actions in so far as they refer to his own developing subjective world, we can make decisions as to the rightness and wrongness of actions which appear to affect other people. Nevertheless even as we do this we must recognize that our judgement is in the context of our own worlds of perception, and must be careful not to rely too much upon purely personal and private elements of those worlds. This is not a particularly novel viewpoint. The impossibility of judging 'sin', and the necessity of protecting society by means of law, has long been recognized. Nevertheless it is interesting to notice that poetry does imply, by its mode of procedure, this particular paradox.

We are concerned, however, with poetry as ethics. Here Berdyaev has expressed the creative viewpoint most clearly. A series of quotations will, perhaps, put the attitude most clearly.

One ought always to act individually and solve every moral problem for

[1] Pierre Emmanuel, *The Universal Singular*, trans. Erik de Mauny, Grey Walls Press, 1950, p. 198.
[2] John Dewey, op. cit., p. 103.
[3] Pierre Emmanuel, op. cit., p. 252.

oneself, showing creativeness in one's moral activity, and not for a single moment become a moral automaton. A man ought to make moral inventions with regard to the problems that life sets him.

The ethics of creativeness takes a very different view of the struggle against evil than does the ethics of law. According to it, that struggle consists in the creative realization of the good and the transformation of evil into good, rather than in the mere destruction of evil.

The ethics of creativeness is concerned with revealing human values and the value of human personality as such, and in doing so it frees man from the unendurable fear for himself and his future—the fear which gives rise to idolatry and superstition . . . Creative inspiration is a way to victory over fear which, owing to original sin, is the ruling emotion of life. At moments of creative elation an artist or a man of science becomes free from fear . . .

The ethics of creativeness alone overcomes the negative fixation of the spirit upon struggle with sin and evil and replaces it by the positive, i.e., by the creation of the valuable contents of life. It overcomes not only the earthly but the heavenly, transcendental selfishness with which even the ethics of redemption is infected. Fear of punishment and of eternal torments in hell can play no part in the ethics of creativeness. It opens a way to a pure disinterested morality, since every kind of fear distorts moral experience and activity. It may indeed be said that nothing which is done out of fear, whether it be of temporal or of eternal torments, has any moral value. The truly moral motive is not fear of punishment and of hell, but selfless and disinterested love of God and of the divine in life, of truth and perfection and all positive values. This is the basis of the ethics of creativeness.

But love can only transform evil passions into creative ones if it is regarded as a value in itself and not as a means of salvation. Love in the sense of good works useful for the salvation of the soul cannot give rise to a creative attitude to life and be a source of life-giving energy. Love is not merely a fount of creativeness but is itself creativeness, radiation of creative energy.

To transcend the morality of law means to put infinite creative energy in the place of commands, prohibitions, and taboos.

The creative act is an escape from time, it is performed in the realm of freedom and not of necessity. . . . The creative image is outside the process of time, it is in eternity.[1]

[1] Nicolas Berdyaev, *The Destiny of Man*, trans. Natalie Duddington, Geoffrey Bles, 1937, 1954 edn. pp. 126–53.

Berdyaev's view is dependent upon a philosophical and theological system of ideas which has as its basis a belief in Christ and a particular attitude towards the nature of man. We may be able to accept his attitude towards ethics as one which can result also from an exploration of the values presented by poetry. Whether or not poetry leads us to agreement with his other beliefs is doubtful. It is, however, useful to examine some of his statements about the nature of man and the purpose of existence, for he is clearly in sympathy with the creative attitude of the artist, and, by means of his formulations, we may be able to see our own investigations in a different light.

We can start by observing that in the passages we have quoted he has indicated love as the building principle of morality. He has identified love with creativity in much the same way as we did in an earlier chapter. He has also indicated that his ethics are based upon a strong feeling for the uniqueness of each individual and each individual situation. This feeling is one which we have also seen as a basic element in the poetic attitude. It is his final statement concerning eternity which raises new problems, however, and this faces us yet again with the problem of time. Let us examine first of all his attitude towards man, and then try to come to some conclusion about the nature and function of time.

Berdyaev states that 'Truth is apprehended not by abstract, partial man who is referred to as reason, mind in general and universal spirit, but by the whole man, transcendental man, the image of God.'[1] We can agree that the 'whole man' is the perceiver of truth. We have been saying this all along, and we have argued that it is in poetry that the 'whole man' is brought into view. Whether or not he can be described as 'transcendental man' or 'the image of God' is another matter. This knowledge which the whole man reaches is not an objective kind of knowledge. It is participant.

'I am the way, the truth and the life.' What does this mean? It means that the nature of truth is not intellectual and purely cognitive, that it must be grasped integrally by the whole personality; it means that truth is existential.[2]

If we agree that poetry implies this view of the nature of truth, we must also agree that it is opposed to any dogma, and fixed system, and any philosophy which tries to objectify the nature of humanity.

Existential philosophy is expressionist. In other words, it seeks to express the

[1] Nicolas Berdyaev, *Truth and Revelation*, trans. R. M. French, Geoffrey Bles, 1953, p. 20.
[2] ibid., p. 22.

existentiality of the cognitive mind rather than something abstracted from that existentiality, which is what objectifying philosophy seeks to do.[1]

To maintain dogmatically that Truth is something fixed and finished is a very great error. But this underlines both Catholic and Marxist dogma alike.[2]

We can find some support for believing that this is an attitude inherent in the poetic activity by considering the great appeal that all forms of subjective philosophy have always had for poets. At the moment of writing several scholars are busy showing that a great number of English poets have been deeply affected by a subjective tradition based upon neoplatonic thought, upon the use of archetypal symbols, and upon the belief that the concept of a God external to the human personality is incorrect. Yeats, as F. A. C. Wilson has shown, based much of his work upon the view that each life possesses, essentially, its own universe, and took his symbols from religious and philosophical traditions which exalted the self, rather than from 'an orthodox Christianity which deprecated the values of the personality and relied on salvation from without.'[3] Other writers have shown the importance of 'subjective philosophy' to Spenser, Keats, Blake, Coleridge, and Wordsworth. Our concern is not, however, with individual writers, all of whom treated their subjective tradition in different ways; we need only register the fact that a good deal of poetry has been provably based upon philosophical ideas which chime with the conclusions we have reached about the philosophical implications of poetry as such.

Poetry is concerned with human nature, however. Its concept of truth is involved in its concept of humanity, and here Berdyaev can again shed light upon some dark places.

Behind the natural man, and here I include social man, is hidden the man whom I shall call transcendental. Transcendental man is the inner man whose existence lies outside the bounds of objectification. . . . Transcendental man stands outside the division into subject and object and, therefore, all the theories which are derived from knowledge of the object can tell us nothing about him. . . . Transcendental man is not what is called unchangeable human nature, for it is not nature at all. It is creative action and freedom. Neither spirit nor freedom is nature. The nature of man changes, it evolves, but behind it is hidden the transcendental man, spiritual man, not only

[1] ibid., p. 12.
[2] ibid., pp. 23–4.
[3] F. A. C. Wilson, *Yeats's Iconography*, Gollancz, 1960, p. 20.

earthly man but heavenly man also, who is the Adam Kadman of the Kabbalah.[1]

This is a statement we may jib at. Nevertheless we can admit that poetry does go beyond the division into subject and object, and is concerned to present the nature of human perception, which (we dare, perhaps, assume) does not change in any serious way however much other aspects of humanity change and evolve. We can assume this, however, only if we assume that there is some fixity, some steady rock-like principle, in the universe. In other words, if life is not completely a flux, and continually altering in every respect, however slowly, we must assume as one of the fixed principles (perhaps as the only fixed principle) the nature of perception as we have outlined it. This is, however, no more than an assumption, a hypothesis. Berdyaev indicates the importance of making it.

> If the existence of transcendental man may not be admitted, it is impossible to make any pretensions to the knowledge of truth, it is *a priori* to any apprehension of truth. It is not a logical *a priori* or an *a priori* of the abstract reason, it is an *a priori* of the whole man, of spirit. It is the whole man who receives and interprets revelation, not abstract, partial, and merely psychological man.[2]

If we decide to accept 'transcendental man' as a meaningful term, we can certainly see him present in poetry. His existence is postulated by poetry; without him it would be a meaningless activity.

We must now consider this 'whole man', the 'transcendental man' with regard to his relationship to truth. It is he who 'receives and interprets revelation' says Berdyaev. We might prefer to say that it is he who is in a participant relationship with life—with his own construct-system, and with the world of inferred externals. Here we may find it useful to return to the notion of participation and view it from another angle.

We have already noticed that the child lives in a world in which he completely participates. He is involved in all phenomena; it is a world without objects. This is, of course, a state which passes, and yet it is a more real world than the adult one—more real in being more true to the facts of perception. Here is one reason why poetry so often refers back to childhood. Poetry, in attempting to realize, by way of language, a completely participant world, is looking back to childhood. It is also looking forward. It is making the assumption that the complete

---

[1] Nicolas Berdyaev, *Truth and Revelation*, pp. 16–17.
[2] ibid., p. 19.

participation in the world is the end of the human endeavour, and that (in the sense in which we must now understand it after all our explorations) man is constantly trying to become at one with the universe.

Barfield has suggested that the endeavour of man is to achieve a 'final participation' which differs only from the participation of childhood or primitive man in that it is achieved upon the conscious plane as well as the unconscious. Thus poetry is not retrogressive, but progressive. It indicates our goal. 'Revelation as Truth', says Berdyaev, 'presupposes the activity of the whole man, and to assimilate it demands our thinking also.'[1] Or as Dewey has put it in a familiar passage,

Art is the living and concrete proof that man is capable of restoring consciously, and thus on the plane of meaning, the union of sense, need, impulse and action characteristic of the live creature.[2]

This view has some important consequences. If we believe that the end at which man aims is of this kind, then we must oppose his use of means incompatible with that end. We have already seen the 'whole man's' creative view of ethics. What about society in general? Here it is impossible to lay down any positive lines of action, for general laws are likely to be inapplicable to many individuals and, as Blake said, 'One law for the Lion and the Ox is oppression.' We can, however, list some of the aspects of society which poetry, *qua* poetry, finds itself opposing. First of all, it is clear that any form of materialism that assumes a virtue resident in an object rather than in the individual's use of that object is wrong. Secondly, any form of repression, censorship, or inhibition is wrong. Thirdly, any view of history, philosophy, religion, or politics which does not take into account the subjective nature of the universe is wrong. Thus poetry, in essence, is anarchic. If a poet were to base his political beliefs upon his poetry he would be an anarchist, though (obviously, as respect for others is an integral part of the poetic attitude) a syndico-anarchist rather than a nihilist.

We do not, however, live in a world in which such attitudes are practicable. They are impracticable simply because not everyone is ruled by the poetic system. Nevertheless, a large part of the distrust of the arts which is so often expressed or implied by organs of public or official opinion is the result of an instinctive appreciation of the anarchic character of art. It is not our business here to show how different

[1] ibid., p. 48.
[2] John Dewey, op. cit., p. 25.

civilizations have tried to either tame or bully the artist. We need not deal with the problem of 'official' art, or art in the service of Church or State. The situation is clear enough. We must, however, examine the less obvious matter of poetry and time. Here it might be as well to adopt the story of the Fall as a framework for our explorations.

The Fall is a valuable myth. It expresses extremely accurately the way in which man (in history and individually) loses his participant attitude. Once we eat of the Tree of Knowledge, which is also the tree of Good and Evil, we fall. That is to say, as soon as we separate ourselves from the world, and recognize a distinction between subject and object, we are required to make moral judgements.

The recognition of subject and object, the recognition of diversity, is a product of the time-sense. The birth of time can be regarded as a concomitant of the Fall. In a purely subjective world there is no time. In a world of objects there is. Without time there could be no objects, no data, only existence. Existence can only be a condition, not an activity. Existence cannot progress. Activity requires a sense of relativity, and demands the possibility of making new dispositions of given material. Thus time is necessary. Without time no new dispositions could be made. The very word 'new' depends for its meaning upon an apprehension of time.

Time is, therefore, a mechanism that enables activity to take place. Time also, however, results in a sense of 'otherness'. It forces us to set one thing against another, and to see some things as being near to us, others as far from us. It requires us to perceive relationship. We thus extend our 'constructs' outside ourselves in order to place them in relationship with other constructs. We are obliged to infer a world external to ourselves as percipients. This means that if we 'construct' other percipients, we are able to communicate with them in terms of other inferred externals. Thus time enables communication to take place (or, if you prefer it) the sense of communication to exist. This communication can, however, only be complete, or felt as complete, if it involves the sense of participation. Participation itself requires the sense of otherness. Without 'otherness' participation is an impossible concept. Therefore time can be regarded as a mechanism enabling participation to take place—even making it inevitable. The deepest and most complete form of participation is love. Thus time can be regarded as a strategy of love. And love is itself the full use of the strategy, and recognizes its strategic function in returning us to a fuller apprehension of our true reality. It is not a very big step from this point to suggest that in observing this process we recognize that we are both the creator of our world and an inhabitant of it, being present in every construct, and yet also being the originators of those constructs. This observation can lead directly to the constructing of a God whose process of construction, externalization, and participation parallels our own. It can also, equally, lead to the denial of a God. One can argue that it is simply because we find our situation uncomfortable, being ourselves responsible for our lives, that we must create a God who does not in fact exist. Yet the idea of God is inevitable, and whether we label the idea as false or true, it exists as an element of our subjective worlds of perception.

Whatever attitude we adopt towards God as Creator, however, we are likely to recognize that love, as the most complete form of participation, is the most creative complex of emotion, intuition, senses, and intelligence, which we know is an important principle. It is not only the poet's desire always to unify the personality which causes him to deal frequently with sexual love, and to postulate the existence of a Muse. It is also his perception of a guiding principle within the poetic system of values. Again, it is often noticeable that poetry which is used in the service of any orthodox religion is very rarely expressive of dogma, as such. Poetry finds the concept of God, or of Gods, important, and cannot avoid dealing with it. The relationship of the individual with the idea of God is also the relationship of the individual with ideas of fundamental unity, complete participation, and universal order, and these are notions central to poetic perception.

Be that as it may, we must return to an earlier suggestion of Berdyaev. He described the 'creative image' as being 'in eternity'. If our view of the function of time is anything like true, this statement can now be regarded as meaningful. Poetry, by unifying our perceptions in terms of a world of participation, and by returning us to a world in which the distinction between subject and object is only made use of in order to communicate experientially a perception of the whole or transcendental man, to whom the word 'object' has no real meaning, is indeed operating in an eternal fashion.

It is also operating in eternity in a different way. Pierre Emmanuel wrote:

> To be contemporary with the eternal means that every man is contemporary with every other, and communicates even without being aware of it between one point and another in the destiny of humanity. History, as seen by the universal mind, is both a successive explanation and a simultaneous revelation. . . . What we call immortality is not only our state after death, but our

individual presence in every man, a presence of which we suspect neither the intensity not the extent.[1]

This statement, like many in this chapter, comes near to regarding poetry as a form of religion. Certainly poetry does imply attitudes which can be described as religious. M. Emmanuel, in fact, sees the poet's task in religious terms:

> . . . our responsibility before words is identified with our freedom in history, and the effort of reflection which raises art to its final heights is inseparable from the will to salvation: it is a knowledge of man in the permanent form of his present destiny, a prescience of the abysses into which a misinterpretation of his nature might drag him, a mobilisation of those inner energies which will divert him from the threat by which he is fascinated.[2]

In opposing worship of the merely analytical intelligence M. Emmanuel re-states some of our earlier conclusions in his own terms:

> . . . enslaved as we are by analytical methods, in abandoning them we quake to lose the virtue of intellect. But when it has once become clear that unitary or symbolic thought has no intention of demonetizing understanding, but of integrating analysis itself in a vaster logical effort, nothing will be able to prevent a promotion of the symbolic faculty to reason, and a cessation of that secular disfavour which condemns it to go begging, in the tawdry finery of hermeticism, the indulgence of dreamers alone.[3]

This does, perhaps, indicate the profound idealism of poetry. The poem is an act of faith. It assumes that man can become fully integrated, and that he can learn to recognize his own nature, and his modes of perception.

> . . . when consciousness, rejecting its pretended objectivity, becomes passion and will, when it selects, reduces and disciplines its symbols, its own structural effort liberates it. Having a foothold on the common basis of mankind, it senses the biology of history, the knowledge of which may perhaps deliver man from time. By extrapolating the curve it traces, it conceives, beyond its relative transcendence, the existence of a transcendent absolute. Art, at the summit of consciousness, becomes morality and religion.[4]

. We have now arrived at a word which everyone will interpret in a different way, and a statement which arouses far more questions than it answers. This is perhaps appropriate in a book which has, all the time,

[1] Pierre Emmanuel, op. cit., p. 148.
[2] ibid., p. 183.   [3] ibid., p. 198.   [4] ibid., p. 124.

been concerned less to provide water-tight answers than to explore speculations. At the point at which it is felt that art approximates to a religion we are face to face with the poet himself, animated by a sense of vocation, and dominated by a belief in the limitless importance of the job he is doing. We have, in fact, reached the point at which it becomes important to emphasize that those conclusions we have reached are the conclusions of one individual poet, and can only be of value if they are tested against experience by each individual reader. After all, one of the main arguments of this book has been the ultimate privacy of each person's picture of the universe, and the picture this book presents can hardly be regarded as an exception to the rule.

It is impossible to conclude with a summary of all that has gone before. Our explorations have been attended by so many qualifications, hypotheses, arguments and counter-arguments that any attempt at summary would certainly fail. One or two generalizations might, however, be risked. We have argued that the structure of poetry is, in all respects, an exact presentation of the nature of human perception, and that it conveys to the sensitive reader a remarkably precise picture of the situation of man with regard to his apprehensions of time, history, evolution, language, and the world 'outside' him. We have suggested that poetry, by its very structure, indicates a series of values, and have seen these in terms of the creative ethics of Berdyaev, political anarchism, and the belief in the perfectability of the human 'spirit'. *En route* to these conclusions we have reflected upon the reasons for the situation of the arts in the social scheme of things today, and have been not altogether kind about the academic teaching of poetry and about orthodox religious systems. What remains ?

The answer to that question is obvious. Poetry remains. No matter how many books are written about it, from whatever point of view, poetry itself is always in advance of its commentators. One poet has devoted much of his work to speculation about poetry, and some of his lines may serve us as conclusion. In *An Ordinary Evening in New Haven* Wallace Stevens wrote:

The poem is the cry of its occasion,
Part of the res itself and not about it.
The poet speaks the poem as it is,

Not as it was: part of the reverberation
Of a windy night as it is, when the marble statues
Are like newspapers blown by the wind. He speaks

By sight and insight as they are. There is no
Tomorrow for him. The wind will have passed by,
The statues will have gone back to be things about.

The mobile and the immobile flickering
In the area between is and was are leaves,
Leaves burnished in autumnal burnished trees

And leaves in whirlings in the gutters, whirlings
Around and away, resembling the presence of thought,
Resembling the presences of thoughts, as if,

In the end, in the whole psychology, the self,
The town, the weather, in a casual litter,
Together, said words of the world are the life of the world.[1]

[1] Wallace Stevens, op. cit., p. 473.

Index

Index

Q4